A legacy of speed.

THE
GEE
BEE
RACERS

Charles A. Mendenhall

SPECIALTY PRESS

Books by Charles A. Mendenhall
The Air Racer
The Gee Bee Racers: A Legacy of Speed

First Printing—September 1979

ISBN 0-933424-05-1
LC #79-19175

Library of Congress Cataloging in Publication Data

Mendenhall, Charles A.
    The Gee Bee racers.

    Bibliography: p. 174
    Includes index.
    1. Gee-Bee (Racing plane) 2. Granville
Airplane Company, Springfield, Mass.   I. Title.
TL685.6.M453   629.133'343   79–19175
ISBN 0-933424-05-1

Published by: Specialty Press Publishers and Wholesalers, Inc.
            North Branch, MN 55056

Cover: Photo credit Gerald Liang.
    First lift-off of the Turner Gee Bee Model Z replica, December 1978

For Diane

Contents

Drawings

The Macchi M-39, flown by
Major Mario DeBarnardi,
won the 1926 Schneider
Trophy Race at 246.5 miles
per hour. Race was held at
Hampton Roads, Virginia.

Warren M. Bodie

The Supermarine S-6B
finally retired the Schneider
Trophy to England in 1930.
Craft later set world speed
record of 406.9 miles per
hour in 1931.

Supermarine

The Macchi–Castoldi MC-
72, powered by a 24-cylin-
der 2800-horsepower Fiat
A.S.6, set the world speed
record for seaplanes in
1933 at an amazing 440.681
miles per hour. It still
stands today.

Macchi Photo

Introduction

THE GEE BEE RACERS were fast, colorful, and cursed with the most outrageous bad luck imaginable. They were also much, much more. Until their remarkable but brief time span in aviation history, no other aircraft ever made such daring contributions to the advancement of speed, to the amazement of thousands, and to the excitement and adventure of American ingenuity in full bloom.

At the time the Gee Bee series was begun, not thirty years had passed since the stick and wire Wright *Flyer* had taken to the air for a one-hundred-twenty-foot flight across the windswept dunes of Kitty Hawk. Any invention of a transportation device soon results in a race, and the airplane was no different. By 1909, less than six years after the first successful heavier-than-air flight, an international speed contest was held at Rheims, France. Glenn Curtiss took over the meet with his *Golden Flyer* fluttering along at a little over forty-six miles per hour and emerged an international celebrity.

With the exception of the World War I years, this contest, the James Gordon Bennett Cup, was destined to run through 1920 as an annual event. Under the impetus of competitive racing and, of course, prize money, the races quickly brought about the introduction of the Depperdussin and Nieuport monoplanes. They were a quantum jump in structural design and speed over the crude bamboo and wire Curtiss and Wright aircraft. The early World War I fighters, without a doubt, owed a great deal in design to these fine racing machines.

Since the Bennett races were strictly for landplanes, it wasn't long before a contest became established for seaplanes. In 1912 the Schneider Trophy Race held its first annual event. This contest was not to be finally settled until 1931. It required that a country win three of these contests in a row before the cup could be permanently retired. The ultimate winner, the Supermarine S–6B, powered by a Rolls-Royce engine, finally took the cup for England with a speed of 340 miles per hour. It then went on to set a world's speed record over a measured course at 406.997 miles per hour later that same month. If that speed seems high, it should be remembered that for seaplanes unlimited runways existed. Large, miles-long bays and river mouths enabled them to have extremely high weight-to-wing-area ratios. Try that with a landplane and a pilot would have more than his hands full with even the two-mile-long jetways of today, particularly without flaps, brakes and reversible-pitch propellers. None of these had been invented yet.

During the 1920's, in the United States at least, the military services were to compete in a series of races for the newly created Pulitzer Trophy. Held as an annual event, they polished the pylons with a variety of aircraft, mostly biplanes, using service lieutenants and captains as pilots. Far greater government funds than could be raised by a private citizen kept individual design efforts in the background. A few tried to enter but they were lost in the shuffle. Nineteen twenty-five was the last of the Pulitzer Races, but the National Air Races were formed in their stead. The first was in 1926. Again, the special military speed machines were the major competitors in the realm of high-speed flight.

However, in the Thompson Cup Race, a free-for-all held in 1929, that all suddenly changed. Doug Davis, flying the Travel Air *Mystery Ship* with superb pilotage, blasted his way around the Cleveland race course leaving the military biplanes in his wake. The Army and Navy were chagrined at the drubbing they took from the civilian upstart, and that was the end of their participation, except for Captain Arthur Page's ill-fated entry in the 1930 Thompson.

This win by a gutsy civilian builder heralded the beginning of the Golden Age of air racing. The period was to extend through 1939, with the Nationals having all the popularity and pizzazz of the Indy 500. The National Air Races at Cleveland were a week-long Labor Day extravaganza of aerial thrills, spills and big press. The dazzling performance of the Gee Bee Model Z in 1931 and the Gee Bee R–1, flown by Jimmy Doolittle in 1932, added to the fantastically thrill-charged aura of the contests. These tournaments of aerial hot rods continued through 1939; the last race was held the day Hitler's war machine moved on Poland. Public heroes and their hell-for-leather speedsters, such as Wedell in 44, Howard in *Mr. Mulligan*, Kling in *Jupiter, Pride of Lemont,*

The Travel Air Model R *Mystery Ship* won the 1929 Thompson Trophy Race at 194.9 miles per hour. With Doug Davis piloting the ship, it marked the beginning of the Golden Age of air racing.

Beech

and the aerial showman of all time, Roscoe Turner, in the LTR Special, had moved through the thirties leaving a legacy of speed for the warplane builders.

The blood bath that overtook the world through 1945 stopped all air racing, but when the last, sad love songs of war had been sung on the "Lucky Strike Hit Parade," it began again. However, with the spectacle of a daily dose of the world conflict still on its mind, the public's taste had become jaded, and who could blame them. Though the pilots and aircraft continued to dust the pylons, racing on the scope of the thirties just never caught on again. Though the annual air races at Reno and Mojave still exist today, they are mainly for the gratification of the participants and a few thousand interested spectators. In retrospect, the absolute high point of this most demanding of motor sports was the winning of the 1932 Thompson Trophy Race by the man/machine team everybody remembers, Jimmy Doolittle and the Gee Bee R-1.

This book, then, is to chronicle the beginning, the background, the rise to superstar fame, and the demise of the legendary Gee Bee machines.

It is a story of the American scene as can only be played by men and women with guts, ingenuity, perseverance and generally no bankroll.

This book is dedicated to the many fine researchers who through the years have generously shared their knowledge, photos and records with me. That interest on their part has finally resulted in this volume. Where possible, photographs have been credited to their origins. Otherwise, they have been attributed to the collection from which they came.

Charles 'Speed' Holman took the 1930 Thompson Trophy Race in this biplane bomb, the Laird LC-DW-300 Solution, at 201.91 miles per hour.

W. Yeager

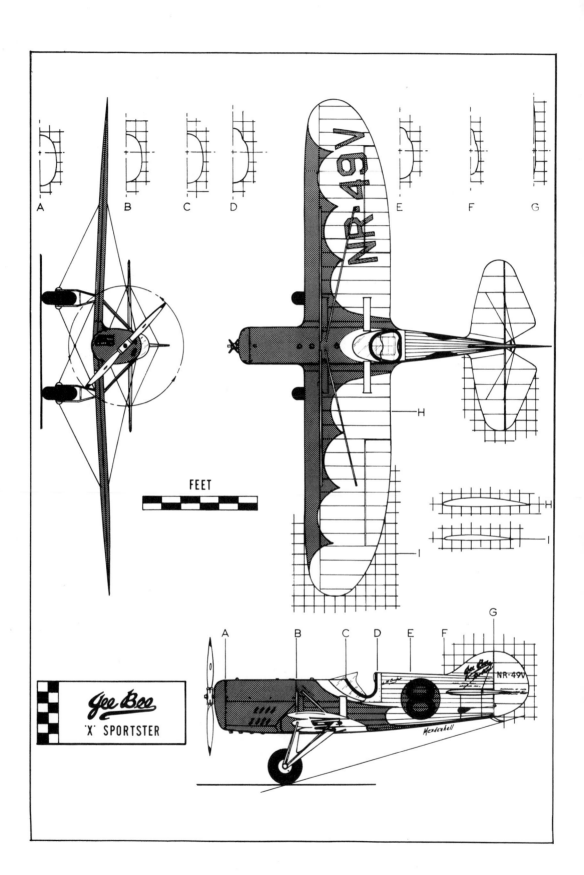

FEET

Gee Bee
'X' SPORTSTER

1

Biplanes and Sportsters

ZANTFORD GRANVILLE came from craggy Madison, New Hampshire. Lean, like the land he was from, Zantford, a typical New Englander, was deeply infused with that well known ingredient: Yankee ingenuity. He went through eight grades in the puritanical local school, better than par for the course for small-town males in the early 1900's. By the time he reached his teens he had invented and constructed a wooden bicycle, a gasoline-engine-propelled water-well windlass, and an adding machine, among other mechanical creations to his credit. A self-taught mechanic, he was so good that at nineteen he successfully operated his own garage in Arlington, Massachusetts— that showed some real gumption.

While he accomplished this, 'Grannie,' as he was affectionately called by all who knew him, had a better idea. Aviation, created in stick and wire by the Wrights, nurtured by the compelling forces of World War I, and perfected to a relatively high degree in the twenties, drew Grannie's interest like a magnet attracts a nail. This was a little strange, as he was afraid of heights. A trip to the top of the barn roof supposedly paralyzed him with fear for days.

A way out of the auto repair garage business was to talk his brother Tom into coming to Arlington and running the place. That freed Grannie to go to the East Boston Airport and get involved in the interesting world of aviation. His natural mechanical aptitude stood him in good stead. He soon found work as a mechanic on both engines and airframes. He also finally took his first airplane ride in an old Curtiss and loved it. With some money coming in from Tom, who was holding the fort at the Arlington garage, Grannie was able to trade his mechanical acumen for flying lessons. He took to flying with a natural talent like a duck to water, and in 1925 he obtained his pilot's license. It was a ticket to a feeling of self achievement, fulfillment, fame and, in the end, abrupt death less than ten years later.

Now that he had learned to fly, Grannie wanted to stay in the game. What then? Even today, this is a problem for fledglings once they get their wings. Granville knew what to do. What goes up, comes down—and sometimes hard! Since he had been doing mechanic's work on the East Boston fleet anyway to supplement his income, and had also built a pretty good name for himself . . . well, going into his own business was the obvious answer. 'You wreck 'em, we fix 'em,' has been the basis for the establishment of countless hundreds of businesses in the American system of free enterprise.

The East Boston Airport's legal status was in some question—it was just a flat hayfield and no permanent buildings were available. That was good and bad. It was good because no one else had a clean, efficient repair hangar to compete with him, and bad—because he didn't have one either. A flatbed truck was the answer. Not being that well-off, the real answer was to purchase an old car and make a flatbed truck out of it. This was a typical Granville 'mother of invention' solution to the problem.

The rolling repair shop, equipped with aviation mechanic's tools, steel tubing, wire, plywood, canvas and bamboo, was ready for anything. It was an instant success. With a roaring aircraft repair business on his hands, he quickly added a second smaller truck and had Tom Granville close the Arlington garage and come join him in the heady economic climate at the East Boston Airport. That still was not enough, so he brought in the whole Granville brother contingent, adding Robert, Mark and Edward. The name of the repair firm became Granville Brothers Aircraft; hence came the name Gee Bee that was to thrill a million people in the coming years.

Things were going great. Cylinder heads got pulled and rebuilt, valves ground, plugs changed, smashed wing tips made new again, tires and control cables replaced and any other repair that was wanted was quickly and efficiently attended to. This was all fine and great, but there wasn't much room for invention there, just fixing them. However, the constant fixing showed one thing: There was a lot of room for improvement on the airplanes of the twenties.

By the early morning of May 3, 1929, the inevitable had come to pass. Inventive Grannie had built an original aircraft, the first of the Gee Bee line. At 5:30 A.M., with clouds scudding and lightning flashing from nearby thunderstorms, Grannie Granville made the maiden flight. His brothers were the sole audience. Even though the weather was inclement and it was early in the morning, everyone was wide awake for this one. Many hours and most of their money was tied up in the project. The purpose of the clandestine test hop was simple enough: they didn't want any outsiders to witness a failure—and there wasn't one! It was a good thing, too—there was no parachute either!

The ship had several interesting features, such as a stick that came from beneath the control panel, then bent at right angles to form a horizontal handle. This gave more leg room.

A full-span flap arrangement utilized the whole upper wing to lower the landing speed somewhat. The craft had a span of twenty-seven feet and a wing area of 200 square feet. It had a landing speed of forty, a cruising speed of ninety and a top speed of 108 miles per hour when eventually it was powered by a Kinner K–5 engine.

When the first flight became known, as well as its success, the Boston newspapers hailed it mightily. It was the first Boston-built aircraft. The Granvilles touted the Gee Bee Model A as "a business, sport or training airplane offering the utmost in comfort, safety and dependability." The uncluttered, roomy side-by-side cockpit was easily accessible. The large windshield, deep cushions, large baggage compartment, and oil and rubber shock struts also added to the plane's attractiveness. Having been handcrafted by expert artisans, the final product showed beautiful workmanship and finish.

The airplane was of normal construction for the period: spruce spars and Clark Y ribbed wings that were fabric covered, and a welded, steel tube fuselage that was also fabric covered over spruce stringers and plywood formers. There was an aluminum covering around the engine and cockpit. The powerplant on the original test flight was a Velie M–5 engine that could, on a good day, deliver sixty horsepower. The prototype during its career eventually carried at least two other engines, a Chevrolair D–4 and a Cirrus Ensign. The aircraft was also fitted with floats and skis at various periods.

A Gee Bee Model A biplane on the line. One of eight built, it had a Kinner engine.

T. C. Weaver Collection

It was the beginning of the famous Gee Bee scalloped paint scheme on the wings and fin. Other niceties included wheel brakes and a full-swiveling tail wheel, with a flat on its spindle, to hold it rigidly in place during landings and take-offs. Most other contemporary aircraft did not have these features. Also, by design, many parts were interchangeable, such as wing panels, landing gear legs, and wing struts. All in all, though squat and a little dumpy-looking, the Gee Bee Model A biplane didn't have to take a back seat to any of its apron-mates.

One thing was certain, even with a tested good design for a business/sport biplane, they were not going to be able to produce any quantity of the product outdoors beside a flatbed truck at the East Boston Airport.

Within two weeks of the first flight, after checking several municipal chambers of commerce, they came up with some solid support. On May 16, 1929, the Springfield, Massachusetts, Chamber of Commerce gave them a break. The four Tate brothers, who were big in ice cream and dairy products as well as financial champions of the Springfield Airport's opening, offered monetary backing.

With money, a design, and great enthusiasm, the new organization, Granville Brothers, Incorporated, moved into a

The Gee Bee biplane as shown in Gee Bee sales literature of 1930. Aircraft shown had Kinner engine.

Granville Brothers Aircraft

former dance hall pavilion located on the edge of the Springfield Airport in late July, 1929, and Zantford Granville was named president.

Wood and metal-working equipment was immediately procured and production commenced. All was well, except it wasn't—the Great Depression was on its way to wreak economic chaos on the country and the world. Banks closed, stock brokers did themselves in and the Granvilles found they couldn't sell airplanes. The Model A biplane was to see production through only eight units.

Since the biplane was a dead issue, the company turned its attention to the idea of building custom aircraft for wealthy sportsmen pilots who could still afford the luxury of flying. However, as 1929 drew to a close, the prospects for the company, while not impossible, offered little except gloom. One bright spot was Bob Hall, a very talented designer, who had joined the group during the year and would certainly be useful going into the custom design business. Hall was also an excellent pilot. As the snows of a Massachusetts winter began to fall lightly on the dance pavilion, a letter arrived that was to change the course of events with the company forever.

The letter contained a two-page spread with the words, "The Twenty Five Thousand Dollar All American Flying Derby" emblazoned across the top. Sponsored by American Cirrus Engines, of Marysville, Michigan, it offered a $15,000 first prize, a $7,000 second prize and a $3,000 third prize.

The rules of the race were relatively simple. The race was to be flown by planes powered with either American Cirrus or American Ensign Hi-Drive engines with or without a DePalma supercharger. The supercharger could increase performance from ninety to 110 horsepower. The race was to start from Detroit on July 21, 1930, with a long 5,541-mile course taking the entrants over every kind of terrain and through every type of flying conditions that could be found on the North American continent. Detroit, Montreal, New York, Dallas, Los Angeles, Omaha, Chicago and back to Detroit was the route of the race.

Pilots were required to wear parachutes and make a controlled stop each night and start at a fixed time each morning with the longest daily flight being about 900 miles. The winners would be determined by the total flying time elapsed between control points.

"That could do it," mused Grannie, drawing thoughtfully on his ever-present pipe. If they could place well in the Derby, they could pick up some big prize money and orders would be sure to follow.

Bob Hall, Grannie and the rest put their heads together to come up with a winning design. There was no question about the engine. It would be a supercharged American Ensign Hi-Drive which could churn out 110 horsepower at 2100 rpm's. The package weight was 326 pounds, several pounds lighter than the other engines eligible for the race. The engine was derived from a British design and was license manufactured by American Cirrus Engines, a unit of Allied Motors. Cirrus had used the services of famous race car driver Ralph DePalma in developing a positive, pressure-type supercharger for its engines, raising the horsepower by about twenty percent. Mounted on the rear end of the crankcase and driven at crankshaft speed, the supercharger acted as a damper for crankshaft vibrations in addition to its regular usage. The engine was an air-cooled, four-cylinder inline design.

The airframe was somewhat unique for 1930 which was the age of the biplane for both private and military aircraft. It was low-wing and painted black and white with the now familiar Gee Bee scalloped design used earlier on the Model A biplanes. Its twenty-five-foot span and 16.5-foot length featured a large, comfortable, single-place cockpit. The aircraft was licensed NR–49V. A great deal of this design would still be found years later in the subsequent Gee Bee models. It couldn't be proven by science, but to an artist all the Gee Bee's, except perhaps the biplane, had a distinct flair that made them stand out from the rest. For want of a better name, some called it, "Grannie's built-in tail wind."

A walk around the pert little ship would have revealed the following: An all-metal, ground-adjustable propeller was mounted without a spinner on the Ensign's Hi-Drive crankshaft. The engine was smoothly streamlined by the aluminum cowl which had the usual complement of air intake holes and cooling louvers in the sides. The engine was also rigged for inverted flight by means of a special fuel system. Behind the engine, an oval cross-section fuselage was built up on a welded chrome molybdenum steel tube frame by means of wood formers and stringers. A sheet metal covering was used around the cockpit and on the fuselage top forward of the cockpit. The balance of the fuselage was fabric covered. Protruding from the fuselage frame were welded stubs for attaching the wings and landing gear. The landing gear on this initial model consisted of two V struts, one on either side of the wheel and attached securely to the fuselage frame mounting stubs. Wire bracing, both between the wheels and from the wheels to the outer wing panels, gave the gear lateral stability and strength. Two short struts between the fuselage sides and upper wing surfaces added additional strength to that of the stub spars. Shock absorbing was handled by the fat twenty-by-nine-inch airwheels. A spring steel tail skid completed the landing gear.

The wing was of two-spar construction with a characteristic planform that was to be more or less the same through the Gee Bee Q.E.D., four years and five models later. The leading edge was slightly curved at the tip, blending with the circular wing tip which, in turn, blended into a long, smooth flowing curve that took in nearly half of the trailing edge. The interior of the wing consisted of wooden spars and ribs with wire drag bracing between them. The wings were fabric covered. Streamlined landing and flying wires completed the wing assembly.

The tail, both vertical and horizontal, was wire-braced fabric-covered steel tube framework. The rudder was left unbalanced. Additional features of the Model X included a storage space under the headrest for tools and light luggage. All in all, the Gee Bee Model X was a pilot's airplane, comfortable to fly and no slouch in the performance end either.

The pilot, Lowell Bayles, a slender, quiet Lindbergh-era protogé, was a partner of the Benton-Bayles Flying Service in Springfield. He had kicked over the traces from his student days as a mining engineer by doing the Waldo Pepper bit of learning to fly and, finally, by buying a war surplus Curtiss Jenny. He hopped rides for food and gas, and slept under the wings at times while spending the night in some farmer's pasture. As he grew more experienced, Lowell did some airliner work for the New England and Western Lines in the right seat of a Ford Trimotor as a relief pilot. During this knock-about type of life, he met Roscoe Benton during a barnstorming tour at Tusberg, Florida. The two struck up a good friendship and eventually Bayles returned to Benton's hometown, Springfield, and started the flying service.

At 6:30 A.M. on July 21, 1930, Bayles and the Model X were lined up with seventeen other entries for the Cirrus All American Flying Derby. A fair amount of publicity had been expended and a large crowd from Detroit and neighboring areas had gathered to witness the takeoff. It was a spectacular sight for those days to see engines crackling to life, billows of blue exhaust smoke drifting pungently in the breeze, and grass flattened behind the planes as whirling propeller blades blended swiftly into silver discs. The planes taxied into position for the starting lineup. Over twenty-five entries had been received for the race, but several had fallen victim to collapse, either financial or structural. In addition to Bayles and the Model X, the following aircraft and pilots were about to embark on the 5,541-mile journey over the airlanes of three countries. Dwarfing the other racers was the Ogden Osprey, a high-wing, six-passenger tri-motor design sporting three ninety-horsepower American Cirrus engines. Designed and built by H. H. Ogden, it was also flown by him. With license number NR–398V, its race number for the derby was 25. It had a wing area of 312 square feet (versus the smallest in the race of seventy-five square feet).

The strangest looking aircraft on the field was the Hosler G&G Special. Quickly designed and built by Russell Hosler and associates, it had taken just twenty-eight days from the first sketches to completion. Compare that to the years it requires for most aircraft to arrive at first test flight status. It was the smallest aircraft in the derby with seventy-five square feet of wing area and it was, to say the least, radical! First of all, the aircraft had only one landing wheel, complete with wheel pant, mounted in the center of the fuselage. Ground stability was provided by skids mounted outboard on the wings. This craft, licensed R–954W with race number 18, also had a retractable wind screen and wing flaps.

Great Lakes biplanes were in profusion at the Cirrus Derby, with five of them having been entered. Some of the best aerobatic aircraft ever, these planes still remain, though on a sporadic basis, in production to the present day. With a maximum speed of only 110 miles per hour, they could not possibly win in the Derby; however, the publicity had to be good for the sales of this splendid biplane trainer. Statistics include a span of twenty-six feet eight inches; a length of twenty-six feet four inches; and an empty weight of a little over 1,100 pounds. One of the five entered was cleaned up by Charles W. Myers, a Great Lakes test pilot, and achieved slightly better performance. The other four were stock and flown by W. H. Holliday, W. H. Cahill, Joseph Meehan and Cecil Coffrin.

One of the first true Cessna racers was entered: the Cessna GC–1. Influenced by the $25,000 prize money of the Derby, the Clyde V. Cessna Aircraft Company of Wichita, Kansas, designed and built this aircraft for a group of businessmen from Blackwell, Oklahoma. The bright red cantilever mid-wing racer carried license number NR–144V and was awarded race number 16. It was named *Miss Blackwell* after the company that had put up the $250 entry fee for the Derby, Blackwell Aviation. It was piloted by Stanley Stanton, who had aided in the building of the racer. When it arrived in Detroit, the racer was

The Gee Bee Model X Sportster was the first low-wing model. It was first fitted with an American Cirrus Hi-Drive engine producing 110 horsepower. Top speed was 145 miles per hour.

T. C. Weaver Collection

immediately dubbed "the winged torpedo" by the press and billed as one of the top three contenders in the Derby. The craft was powered by a 310-cubic-inch Cirrus supercharged engine.

A man yet to gather the complete fame and idolization he wound up with in later years at the National Air Races was Jimmy Wedell, whose '44' racing aircraft as well as the famous Roscoe Turner record-breakers which he flew were yet to be heard from. He had already built two larger racers that year (1930), but his entry was the *We Will Jr.*, race number 17—it was still another shot at some prize money. Licensed NR–10337, the scarlet fuselage and silver wings still needed pants on the treadle gear to make the ship as sleek as its sister ships would be at the Thompson and Bendix races to come. Though he had lost the sight of one eye in a motorcycle accident, Wedell showed no sign of this handicap, and most people didn't realize the problem. Before this race, he was supposedly considered just an air hobo from Texas where he had spent some time profitably running guns to Mexico. This little racer was important, for within a year the Wedell-Williams organization would lock horns with the Granville Brothers for both prize money and public adulation.

The Model X at Little Rock, Arkansas, during the Cirrus All American Flying Derby; its black and white Gee Bee paint scheme shows clearly.
T. C. Weaver Collection

An old chestnut for the race was a de Havilland Moth flown by J. Kruttschmitt. This staid, elderly biplane trainer had made its first flight in 1925, so it was definitely not designed for this race. With a span of thirty feet and a length of 23 feet 8½ inches, the maximum speed of this stringbag creation was only 98.5

miles per hour. Still, it added a little international flavor to the proceedings.

Another strong contender in the race was the red Commandaire *Little Rocket*, built by the Commandaire Company of Little Rock, Arkansas. The craft was piloted by Lee Gehlbach, who later was to become a figure of stature within the Gee Bee organization. For the air racer buff, it bore a striking resemblance to the Howard *Pete* aircraft, also powered by a Cirrus engine. This low-wing job was a real beauty. With a span of twenty-four feet six inches, and a length of twenty feet two inches, she weighed in at a slim 740 pounds empty. She would be a first-rate contender. The race number was 1 and it was licensed 10403.

Another highly touted and well thought-of aircraft in contention was the biplane designed and built by Matty Laird that was flown by Herman Hamer. Because it was a racing machine,

The third aircraft built in the Sportster series, 855Y was red and white and powered by a 95-horse-power Menasco B-4.
Granville Brothers Aircraft

it was only half the size of the Great Lakes trainers, and this sleek speedster was not too different from the Laird Solution, winner of the 1930 Thompson Trophy Race. *The Vagabond*, as it was called, carried race number 5 and was licensed R–10422 and had a wing area of only 112 square feet.

Larry Brown—codesigner of the Miles and Atwood Special, and designer of the Brown series of racers which included the B–1, B–2 *Miss Los Angeles*, and the B–3 lightweight fighter—had an entry for this race. He designed, built and flew it himself. It was a high-wing, parasol-type craft with the long graceful fuselage style of the later *Miss Los Angeles*; called the *California Cub*, the race number was 4 and it was licensed 337H.

The Alexander Todd racer with race number 23 and licensed R12E was also present and flown by E. B. Todd. During early tests, it was powered by a Chevrolair engine but now, of course, carried a supercharged Ensign Cirrus. A low-wing design, it had two large struts from the top of the fuselage to the upper surface of each wing.

Similar, but much sleeker, was the racer designed by Clayton Folkerts. This early ancestor of the SK–2 *Toots* and SK–3 *Pride of Lemont* was a low-wing bomb that was painted red with race number 6 and licensed NR–500W. 'Stub' Quimby piloted this machine in the race and it was known as the *Mono-Special*. To round out the field, Harvey Mummert, a Curtiss engineer, flew a diminutive Mummert Mercury and B. B. Smith was at the controls of the Pacific School of Engineering Special.

Each day the Derby was to start from the control field at 6:00 A.M., and engines were to be running at 5:30 A.M. The initial takeoff out of Detroit was made in order of the plane's racing number. The numbers had been assigned in the same order as the entry blanks had been received, along with a certified check for $250. The planes were flagged off at fifteen-second intervals with the contestant's time beginning when he started the leg and ending when he crossed a finish line painted across the middle of the field that was designated as the scheduled stop for the day. If, due to some problem, he could not take off at the proper time, the clock started anyway. If he was delayed over six hours, he was automatically disqualified from further participation in the race.

After the first day, new positions were awarded for starting based on the order the aircraft finished the previous day, i.e. the first plane to finish a day's leg would be the first plane off the following morning.

The pilots had to furnish their own lodging, food, gasoline and repairs along the way. The final judging for the three prizes would be on the basis of total elapsed flight time for the entire race.

To quote the Cirrus brochure for the race, it was intended to be "a racking test of airmanship and plane and motor construction, a challenge to American fliers and to American plane designers and builders." It was! Several of the planes that left

Detroit did not return. The G&G Special piloted by Hosler had its single tire blow-out on takeoff out of Cincinnati. The craft was damaged beyond repair for continuing in the race and Hosler was injured. The Folkerts *Mono-Special* nosed over in Arizona. The pilot, Stub Quimby, was not injured but the race was over for him. Jimmy Wedell had new wheel pants fitted to the *We Will Jr.* while in Los Angeles. Now the ship was cleaned up for a really fast run for the money . . . except it didn't happen. On takeoff out of L.A. the engine quit, resulting in a crippling accident and that was it. The sleek little Laird biplane also ran into trouble and did not finish. Lowell Bayles had to make at least one forced landing to repair his plane, the Gee Bee Model X.

When the Derby was finally completed, ten of the original aircraft arrived back in Detroit—eighteen had started. The Commandaire *Little Rocket*, piloted by Gehlbach, had finished first with an average speed of 127.11 miles per hour. On some stretches, with a good tail wind, he moved along with speeds approaching two hundred miles an hour.

The perky little Gee Bee X flown by Bayles was second with an average speed of 116.40 miles per hour. Other finishers included the Ogden Osprey that finished fourth. Brown's *California Cub* was sixth, and the Cessna GC–1 was seventh even though its engine performed miserably during the race. The intake manifold cracked, there were oil and gas leaks, and push rods and exhaust stacks gave up. There was a wheel collapse and even, at one point, the loss of all his navigational

The tan and brown Model B Sportster was similar to the X except for shock absorber, landing gear and more streamlined fairing.

Granville Brothers Aircraft

instruments—talk about perseverance. The Alexander Todd Special also finished, but in last place.

American Cirrus pointed out in its literature before the race that, for the pilot, the race offered opportunity to win personal glory as well as substantial pecuniary rewards. For the planes, designers and builders (or manufacturers), it offered the opportunity of proving his product before the public in a manner not only spectacular and thrilling but, above all else, convincing. The statement was true, for Bayles collected the $7,000 second prize money and a fair degree of notoriety—especially in aviation circles. Granville Brothers Aircraft, in turn, made a substantial impact on the aviation world with the Model X. Since the winner, the Commandaire *Little Rocket*, was a one-of-a-kind aircraft, the Model X became the only production plane that was a winner in the prestigious Derby to be offered for sale to the general aviation public. Here was a grandly proven design that offered reliability, safety and speed to the sportsman pilot.

It wasn't long before orders began to appear and further models of the X were built—eventually nine in all. Bayles bought the black and white Derby aircraft for his own use. Subsequent models were referred to as Model D for the inline engine versions and Model E for those fitted out with radial engines. Five different engines were to be married to these various airframes during the course of their careers. These were the 125 horsepower C-4 Pirate, the 130 horsepower Ranger 6-390, the 95

Painted light blue and cream, this Model D Sportster was the personal aircraft of Zantford 'Grannie' Granville for a time. It was the fifth Sportster aircraft produced and was Menasco-powered.

T. C. Weaver Collection

horsepower Menasco B–4 and, of course, the inline 110 horse-power supercharged Cirrus Ensign. The Warner Scarab radial was used in the E models, and it delivered 110 horsepower. Rudder and fin area were a little larger for the inline engine versions of these aircraft to make up for the additional wetted side area of that type powerplant. As a result, the inline Model D aircraft was seventeen feet three inches long versus the radial jobs where the length was sixteen feet nine inches. Landing gear also progressed in design to a full-panted treadle gear

This Model E was painted red and white. It was the aircraft in which Russell Boardman was injured just before the 1932 National Air Races.
Collection Photo

'Mother Goose' with two goslings, the Model X and a Model E Sportster. Ships were in 1931 Florida State Air Tour.
Granville Brothers Aircraft

arrangement as the models were developed. Other more specific data for these aircraft will be found in this book's appendix.

Hall, Grannie and his brothers, along with the other people associated with Granville Brothers Aircraft, enjoyed the temporary prosperity of building more airplanes. However, the depression was snowballing, and they could see it would not be long before the Model X production would go the way of the earlier Model A biplane, and this time they would be out of business. During hard times, sport airplanes were one of the first things people stopped buying.

The 1930 National Air Races had been run, and the winners had collected their prize money. During that year, there had been forty-nine separate events, each doling out money to the winners. Charles 'Speed' Holman had won $5,000 for the big one—the new Thompson Trophy Race. That kind of money was worth going after. Bob Hall approached the Granvilles as to why they shouldn't try for the top prize at the upcoming 1931 Nationals. His competitive spirit was too much to overcome. Lowell Bayles had been to the 1930 Nationals and had taken a fourth place in Event 38, a civilian aerobatic exhibition where he won $300, so he helped Hall fire up the rest of them. It took a while, but it was finally agreed to make a try. They had no choice if they wanted to stay in business.

The wave of the Golden Age of air racing had come, and the Granvilles would ride it for all it was worth.

A green and cream beauty, this Model E was used as a flying billboard for the restaurant named on its side.

C. Mandrake

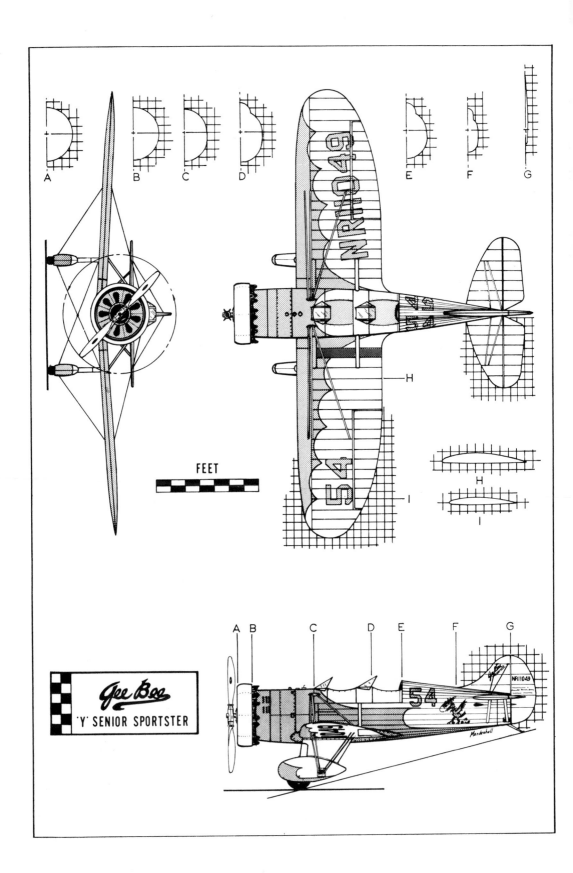

A B C D E F G

FEET

H

I

H
I

A B C D E F G

Gee Bee
'Y' SENIOR SPORTSTER

2

"Z" is for Zinger

THE IDEA OF 'STRETCHING' an aircraft design is thought to be relatively new. In the area of transport design, it has been successfully accomplished many times since World War II. Examples such as the Douglas DC-7, DC-8 and DC-9, and the Lockheed Constellation were all 'stretched.' In each case, a practically new aircraft emerged with much-improved performance and the engineering was considerably less expensive. It was better than beginning a new design program on a blank sheet of paper.

This happened with the basic Granville Brothers Model X, and by the end of 1930 two new aircraft rolled out of the ex-dance hall. They were the Model Y Senior Sportsters and were nearly identical in lines to the radial-engined Model E. However, they sported two cockpits in a longer fuselage, and this change was accompanied by a longer wing span and larger tail surfaces. Licensed 718Y and X11049, the aircraft carried the red and white scalloped design that was to become a Granville trademark, the colors separated by a black pinstripe. Another feature was large, streamlined wheel pants which would also become a familiar Gee Bee trademark. As these planes were developed, they eventually emerged as probably the prettiest, but least radical, of any aircraft ever built by the firm. The proportions were conventionally appropriate for a low-wing airplane, and the effect of the sleekly finished craft was to make the biplane brigade of that era look as archaic as a Wells Fargo stagecoach. An aluminum cover was even provided for the front cockpit, where its windscreen could be stored for high-speed flying.

Like the Model X, the fuselage was internally framed with welded steel tubing that was filled out to contour with fabric covering over plywood formers and spruce stringers. The forward section and the area around the cockpit were covered with sheet aluminum. General dimensions of the aircraft were a span of thirty feet, a wing area of 138 square feet and a length of twenty-one feet.

During the next two years, these airplanes were re-engined several times, starting out with 215 horsepower Lycoming radials, and one of them eventually ended up with a giant 420 horsepower Wright Whirlwind for the 1933 races—an almost one hundred percent increase in horsepower!

It was decided that the planes would be entered in some of the events during the 1931 National Air Races. Howell Miller, who would later take Bob Hall's place as chief engineer, reportedly said in an interview after examining the drawings and the aircraft themselves, "These planes are first rate." The Granvilles also felt they were probably the best product they ever produced.

As Bob Hall looked over both his and the Granvilles' handiwork on the two beautiful racer-like machines, he thought some more about the upcoming 1931 National Air Races, particularly the $7,500 first prize awaiting the winner of the Thompson Trophy Race. Then, too, the money from winning some of the other lesser events wasn't bad either. Looking at the Y, he could visualize using the same basic design, but smaller, built around a big Pratt and Whitney Wasp Jr.

By mid-summer, they had embarked on an all-out program to design a racer specifically to win the Thompson. With Grannie's agreement, Hall now began canvassing everyone in Springfield that might want a piece of the action in this sure-fire new racing machine. This, grimly, required detouring around soup lines at times. He worked day and night sketching and

The Model Y in racing configuration with the front cockpit closed over. Two of these ships were built.

W. F. Yeager

drawing plans for the new plane now labeled Model Z, scarcely staying ahead of the shop's production schedule. To make matters more hectic, money was barely coming in fast enough to pay wages and material expenses. However, the effort gained momentum and the group of shareholders organized into the Springfield Air Racing Association (S.A.R.A.) with James Tait as president. The Model Z was named *City of Springfield, Massachusetts*—a name which would eventually be painted in gold along with a sketch of the city's skyline on the black engine cowling. (The skyline depicted the municipal buildings and included the city hall, auditorium and campanile—a Springfield landmark.)

As planned, the design was based generally on the Model Y and a helpful loan from Pratt and Whitney of a Wasp Jr. hopped up to 535 horsepower. The ultimate goal was to build the smallest, lightest and cleanest airframe possible behind that big radial engine. In an amazingly short time the little bomb took shape, ending up only fifteen feet one inch in length with a diminutive span of twenty-three feet six inches. With the racy enclosed cockpit, large NACA cowl, massive streamlined wheel pants and yellow and black scalloped Gee Bee paint scheme, the Z looked like an overgrown, irate bumblebee. When finally wheeled out of the dance hall/shop on August 22, it appeared to be doing a couple of hundred miles per hour while sitting quietly on the grass.

Starting at the front of the ship, one found an eight foot

The Gee Bee Model Y—a two-place stretched version of the earlier Model D. It was powered by a 215-horsepower Lycoming engine.

W. F. Yeager

two inch Curtiss all-metal fixed-pitch two-bladed propeller, its hub tipped with a bullet-shaped spinner. Driving this prop was the same Wasp Jr. that had pulled the 1930 Thompson Trophy winner—the Laird Solution biplane—to victory. Engine manufacturers enjoyed the publicity given their products when mounted in an air racer. As many components of the Z were direct design derivatives of the Model Y, such was the case with the engine mounts and basic chrome molybdenum welded steel tube fuselage frame. Grannie mentioned, in an article he did about the Z in the October 1931 issue of *Aero Digest*, that "Contrary to the general belief, the Granville Brothers Gee Bee Super Sportster is not a radically new ship in general design and construction. Practically every part is either a duplicate or modification of the standard Gee Bee Super Sportster (Y) two-place job now available commercially."

Wing stub bracing was built as an integral part of the fuselage frame. The fuselage, like that of the Y, was built up to cross-sectional contour over the tube frame by means of plywood formers and spruce stringers. A heavily doped fabric covering then completed the job. The forward fuselage area and around the cockpit were aluminum sheeting.

One new feature the Z had over the Y was the enclosed cockpit covering made up of several pieces of Fiberloid transparent plastic. This allowed the pilot full visibility and, at the same time, protection from the wind at high speed while giving the ultimate in low air-flow resistance. Cockpit ventilation was accomplished by means of tubing that brought in fresh air from the wing stubs and was controlled by a ventilator in the cockpit.

From the forty-six-inch-diameter cowl, the fuselage faired into a gentle outside curve as it progressed rearward until it became flat at the rudder. Granville claimed, when the plump, short-coupled design had received criticism, that the aircraft was based on experience and engineering and was as rigid, maneuverable and stable as its longer-fuselaged contemporaries. Fuel capacity was 103 gallons and it carried eleven gallons of oil. These capacities were somewhat greater than required for the Thompson, but allowed for the possibility that someday they might want to enter the ship in a long cross-country race.

The wings were of all-wood construction and built in two panels, attaching to the stub spars of the fuselage framework with bolts. The two spruce spars were 25½ inches apart with built-up wooden ribs, curved to an M–6 airfoil shape. They were spaced on 5.4-inch centers. X-type drag wires were located between the spars—three sets to a wing. Stewart-Hartshorn landing and flying wires held the wing at its proper dihedral angle. The wire pulls were attached to the compression members to relieve the ribs of all except fabric pressures. Hammered aluminum fillets faired the wings smoothly to the fuselage. Ailerons were of the torque tube type, ball bearing mounted, with sheet steel ribs welded to the torque tube. This beefed-up construction was used to eliminate the danger of flutter and pulling off an aileron, a real disaster in the air.

The landing gear, with six-inch travel on an oil-and-spring shock absorber, was of the treadle fork type. The wheels and brakes were by Aircraft Products Company and carried twenty-three-inch 6.50 x 10 Goodrich tires. The brakes were applied by full back pressure on the stick. The wheel tread was 71¾ inches. Pants and fairings were attached to the wheel forks in a manner that allowed them to travel with the wheel; the wheel and tire were covered in such a way that maximum streamlining was obtained at all degrees of shock deflection. To complete the landing gear, a spring steel leaf-type tail skid was used—the skid streamlined with rubber.

Tail surfaces were fabric-covered welded steel tubing with wire drag bracing and wrapped hinges working directly on the torque tubes. The nineteen-inch-wide rudder was actuated with cables, while the seventeen-inch-wide elevators were operated by a push/pull tube, as well as double cables. Eight feet in span, the stabilizer was moved up and down for trim at the rear by means of a screw-type jack controlled by a crank in the cockpit. It was found later, after testing, that this item was useless as no further setting of the stabilizer trim was needed.

The empty weight of the pudgy little speed demon was 1,400 pounds—2,280 pounds at full gross. This gave a wing loading on the high side, 30.2 pounds per square foot, and a relatively hot landing speed of eighty miles per hour. (Experimental Aircraft Association member Bill Turner has built a replica of the Z. It stalls at 110 miles per hour!) Carrying racing number 4 and license number NR77V, the craft was now ready for the races. A brown pinstripe outlined the numbers and separated the black and yellow main colors.

When the Z was complete and ready to go, Bob Hall took to the air for flight testing and, after a few very minor adjustments, pronounced her ready for Cleveland. The Cleveland National Air Races were scheduled to be held from August 29 through September 7. Since the Z was rolled out on the 22nd of August, it can be seen that a whole lot of time did not exist for test work. This was typical of that period in racer building. In those early days of the Golden Age, as another example, Lee Miles flew the Miles and Atwood Special for the very first time while qualifying it for the Greve Trophy Race—with the paint still wet! Today, the initial flight of a new plane is usually so routine that hardly any interest is generated other than whether it proves out what the computer knew all along. Those early air racer drivers had iron wills and steel nerves.

One man of this type was Lowell Bayles, the slender, quiet young fellow who had piloted the Model X to second place in the All American Flying Derby. Bayles was the pilot elected to fly the Z in the upcoming Thompson Trophy Race—the big one for the Granville group. With an investment of $500, he was also the largest stockholder in the S.A.R.A. This came as somewhat of a disappointment for Bob Hall. He had hoped to race the plane that he had put so much ingenious design into, but as the saying goes, 'money talks.' To soothe Hall's feelings, he was allowed to fly the test work on the Z as well as enter the craft in the Men's and Women's Mixed Invitational Race at the National Air Races in Cleveland. While this race was not as big, it would, at least, allow everyone to see what their speed merchant could do in a closed-course racing event. So off to Cleveland they went, determined to return rich and, of course, famous.

The 1931 Nationals consisted of thirty-eight different events spread out over nine days. The program was arranged to make each succeeding event of greater interest and excitement— just like the Barnum and Bailey Circus.

As it turned out, the Gee Bee products were flown in eight of these events and captured first place in six of them. The other two events garnered second and third places and they too paid prize money. That wasn't too shabby for a company only a little over two years old.

Not only for the Granvilles had things come a long way during the past two years. The National Air Races had attained great stature. They had grown since 1929 to the point that in 1931 a crowd of 37,000 paid to get in, plus thousands of free-loaders attended outside the fences. This occurred on a daily basis as they came to watch the shows of aerial speed.

With American flags and bunting abounding, the opening ceremonies began with pomp and the national anthem. A gaggle of service biplane fighters droned ponderously overhead and the aviation industry, clinging to economic life by a mere thread, loved it and cheered the gigantic air meet on. This group included the people from Granville Aircraft Company and their five products that had showed up for the race. They included three Model D and E Sportsters, a Model Y and, of course, the *City of Springfield* Model Z. These planes emphasized the company's advanced thinking on what a speed plane should look like. The D, E and Y Models were all readily accepted by the spectators and the press as viable aircraft; but the stubby, angry, 'Bumblebee Z' blew everyone's mind. The press, always looking for a feature story, went bananas over the striking and radical little racer. "Much too short coupled," hooted the self-appointed experts. "Who are these Granvilles from the East, and what the hell do they mean causing all the fuss among the more doudy Wedell-Williams and Laird biplanes that are proportioned more like aircraft should be?"

While the Z was getting the lion's share of attention without ever leaving the ground, another Gee Bee, a Sportster Model D powered by a Menasco C–4 engine and flown by Bob Hall, creamed the competition in Event 4, the Men's 400 Cubic Inch Aerol Trophy Cup (A.T.C.) Race, consisting of five laps over a five-mile course. Then, to give the doubters a little food for thought—and a preview of the upcoming Thompson Trophy Race—Bob Hall hopped in the yellow and black Z and took over Event 11 loafing along at 189-plus miles per hour in the

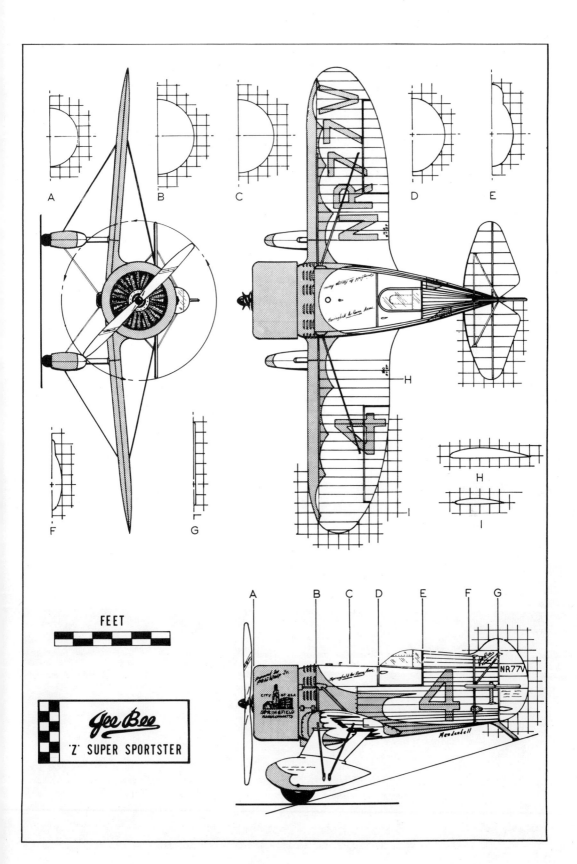

A B C D E

F G

H

H I

I

A B C D E F G

NR77V

FEET

Gee Bee

'Z' SUPER SPORTSTER

25 Mile General Tire and Rubber Men's 1,000 Cubic Inch Race, this time over a Keith Rider and a Wedell-Williams. Lowell Bayles, the Thompson pilot-elect, then took the controls of the Z to try his hand at a small contest in Event 13, the Men's Fifty Mile 1,875 Cubic Inch Free-For-All. Lowell said, "to hell with holding the Gee Bee back," and took the contest at 205 miles per hour, well over fifty miles per hour faster than the next two entries. Jimmy Haizlip was flying a Laird biplane and Benny Howard was flying *Pete*. This was strictly a no-contest situation and, by now, with two easy wins behind them, a real hubbub was created by the press. The fans were jumping up and down for more of this S.A.R.A. entry. Bayles gave them more as he streaked through the Shell Speed Dashes on one run at 286 miles per hour. The world speed record was only 278, and he confided to Grannie that there was still more horsepower in her he hadn't used! In everybody's mind, the way was cleared for Lowell Bayles to really do his thing: win the Thompson. However, before this could be done, three more races had to be run with the now super charismatic Gee Bee progeny.

It was the ladies' turn to try out the remarkable Gee Bee products in pylon competition. In Event 25, the Women's 25 Mile 510 Cubic Inch Free-For-All and Event 26, the Women's 650 Cubic Inch A.T.C. of thirty miles, the results were not as good. Phoebe Omalie of Memphis, Tennessee, with her War-ner-powered Monocoupe, Mae Haizlip of St. Louis and Maude Irving Tait of Springfield, both flying Gee Bees, finished in that

This view of the Z shows off its diminutive size—only a stubby 15 feet 1 inch long with a span of 23 feet 6 inches.

W. F. Yeager

order in both races. Tait, daughter of Granville, backer and S.A.R.A. president James Tait, flew a Model E with a Warner engine, while Haizlip flew a Model D Sportster with a Menasco engine. Even though they took only second and third places in the year-old Sportsters, they came so close to first place that they were, in reality, victims of minute bad luck rather than lack of performance. Maude Tait had already made a name for herself in her own right two years earlier, when she took the family Curtiss Robin to a new unofficial women's altitude record one afternoon when she had nothing better to do.

As activities rolled around to Event 30, the Men's and Women's Mixed Invitational Race of five laps around a ten-mile course, Hall again took to the Model Z and flew it just fast enough to win at 222.6 miles per hour. That beat out Jimmy Wedell in the Wedell-Williams '44' at 221.04 mph and Jimmy Haizlip in the Laird Solution, winner of the 1930 Thompson.

At last, Thompson time came and the boisterous fans reflected the excitement and the suspense. Would that little bumblebee indeed win? The Granville people were a little concerned about how much of the engine they might have used up during the previous two races and Bayles mused on how the Z could be a real handful in some parts of the flight regime.

The most ominous cloud over their chances of winning the Thompson, however, was not the engine in the Z. It was instead a tiny green and yellow Laird Super Solution biplane that had just averaged 223 miles per hour as it sped across the

A nice side view of *City of Springfield* showing off its rakish lines. Note the enclosed cockpit cover is not fitted in this photo. The Z's empty weight was only 1,400 pounds.

T. C. Weaver Collection

country from Burbank to Cleveland to win the first Bendix Trophy Race—and that speed average included fuel stops! On top of that, the pilot of that biwinged speedster was none other than record-breaking, race-winning aviation hero, James H. Doolittle.

The night before the Thompson, the Granville group puttered with the *City of Springfield* for a while, then each turned in and fell into fitful sleep.

The following day found eight racers lined up for the Thompson Trophy Race. Of course, Doolittle was there, bound to have been confident in his Super Solution. In most respects, this aircraft was a direct takeoff of the 1930 Laird Solution piloted by 'Speed' Holman into the winner's circle at last year's Thompson Race. Changes that were evident included the large, streamlined wheel pants; sleeker fuselage streamlining; the engine, hopped up to 535 horsepower; 207 pounds greater weight due

The Gee Bee Model Z was painted black and yellow. 535 horsepower Pratt and Whitney Wasp Jr. pulled the racer along at about 270 miles per hour.

Paramount Studios–Springfield

to the large cross-country fuel and oil tanks; and the installation of complete navigational and blind flying instruments. Doolittle had started from Burbank at 5:30 A.M., and dashed over the Rockies to Albuquerque for fuel stop one, then to Kansas City for stop two and then into Cleveland to claim the Bendix, leaving two Lockheed Orions and two Lockheed Altairs in the dust somewhere back over the continent. Not content with this, he rapidly refueled and dashed off to New York where he clipped an hour and eight minutes off of Lieutenant Commander Frank Hawks' previous transcontinental record. It was then back to Cleveland to collect the prize money and the Bendix Trophy. He was going to be a tough customer to beat.

Another tough customer to beat was Jimmy Wedell in his low-winged, red and white trimmed '44' with the small legend, "Hot as a '44' and twice as fast" painted alongside the racing numerals. The 535 horsepower Pratt and Whitney Wasp, the thin wings only three inches thick, the sleekly faired landing gear, and the gracefully streamlined fuselage showed this entry in the race meant business.

Jimmy Wedell was most formidable as he ascended to his craft's cockpit. He was now bankrolled for a million dollars by Harry Williams of Patterson, Louisiana, and though it was said plans for his machines were drawn with chalk, full size on the shop floor, the end results were still technically something to be reckoned with. As time would reveal, the Wedell-Williams racer series would continue to compete throughout the entire Golden Age of air racing through 1939.

A third contender, 'Red' Dale Jackson, flying the spruced-up Laird Solution biplane could, with a little luck, possibly win. The plane had won the previous year's Thompson.

By far the largest plane in the race was Ira Eaker's Lockheed Altair with a span of forty-two feet nine inches. He had flown it to a lowly fourth place in the Bendix. Benny Howard was flying last year's Howard *Pete*. It was a nice aircraft but much too underpowered to be a serious contender for the Thompson, unless everybody ahead of him flamed out and crash landed—which was always a remote possibility. These lower-powered aircraft were often entered out of their class, however, for mechanical problems, crashes or whatever could sometimes propel them by means of attrition into one of the higher paying prize positions. For the same reason, as long as he could not fly the Z, Hall had entered the Model Y that Maude Tait had flown in earlier events—just in case. Hall had qualified for the Thompson in the Shell Speed Dashes at 213.867 miles per hour. Another hanger-on was William Ong in a Laird Speedwing.

The final entry was the Model Z, to be flown by Lowell Bayles, with the big black '4' emblazoned on its bright yellow sides. He had been testing the Z that morning when the Pratt and Whitney turned sour, forcing him to land. All hands turned out, trying to get her ready for the Thompson; but the quality of the fix added one more worry for Bayles as he now sat at the starting line, engine ticking over and the instrument needles dancing to the vibration. Of course, he was a bit scared. Everything he had was wrapped up in this little bumblebee of an airplane: his cash and maybe even his life, just to get a headline. The volatile grandstands were visible through the canopy. Thousands of people were waiting to see the upcoming battle between the fastest aircraft in the world. The stands were a symphony of colors that would be reduced to a blur the next time he saw it after completing the first lap. He eyed the red and gold trimmed Wedell—not too different from his ship—just a little longer. And there was Doolittle, sitting there with his Pratt and Whitney ticking away in the Super Solution. Those were the two to beat. The rest were just window dressing, the sparrows to pick up what the hawks left behind. With hands a little shaky and moist, limbs a little jerky in anticipation and nervous sweat, there goes the race start! Now it was suddenly all calm, serious business: look for the scattering pylon a mile away and get around it. Doolittle, super pro in a hot airplane, zapped the scatterer and was off to the races with Bayles right behind him. Strung out in the dust astern were Wedell, Jackson, Hall, Eaker, Howard and Ong, in descending order of their aircraft's performance. Doolittle, blasting along at 209 miles per hour, was out front maintaining his lead. Bayles was by now tagging behind. Jackson bashed through a tree top, slowing his Solution's onslaught. Fortunately for Bayles, Doolittle's contention was to be short-lived. He began trailing black smoke from the cowl of the pert little green and yellow biplane, and the Bendix winner began to slow down. Though Jimmy kept the throttle firewalled, a piston had broken under the incessant strain of hours of maximum performance and effort. Bayles, going flat out in the Z, quickly gained the lead over Doolittle and, as he later said, "I knew the race was in the bag." That was, if *he* had no engine problems. Jimmy finally had to land in the seventh lap, and Bayles simply flew on to win the race at a record 236.2 miles per hour. The other ships finished almost as they started; Bayles won $7,500, Wedell came in second winning $4,500, and Dale Jackson took third place and $3,000. With that, the main events of the Nationals were over for another year.

The Kendall Oil Company was to exult the Gee Bee in an ad in the November issue of *Aero Digest* stating: "Lowell Bayles, piloting a Gee Bee Super Sportster, designed and built by Granville Brothers Aircraft, Wasp powered, flashed across the line as winner of the Thompson Classic with an average speed of 236.239 miles per hour. Not content with this splendid victory, another Gee Bee 'Y' plane, piloted by Maude Irving Tait, won the Cleveland Pneumatic Aerol Trophy Race at a speed of 181.574 miles per hour." That pretty well summed up the high spots for 1931 for the Gee Bee gang. The next day, Maude Tait and heroes headed back to Springfield in their now-famous Gee Bee aircraft.

Bayles had done five laps at over 240 miles per hour. The little racer had outdone its competition at the race, but it was yet to break the closed-course record of the Curtiss R2C–1 racer during the 1923 Pulitzer Races. The record stood at 243.7 miles per hour and was flown by the legendary Lieutenant Alford Williams.

All hell broke loose in Springfield that night when the race results became known. The Granvilles were famous, their aircraft were famous, even S.A.R.A. was famous. All this and the S.A.R.A. members got their money back, plus a share of the winnings that gave them a one hundred percent dividend! In this depression-ridden era, a few unexpected extra bucks was a direct gift from heaven. The Springfield Board of Aldermen and City Council passed a Resolution of Commendation. This was to be presented at the airport the next day on the return of the conquerers.

On September 10th at the airport, Maude Tait landed first, followed shortly by Hall, Granville and Bayles. To give the home towners a little show for their pains, Bayles buzzed the field at over 250 miles per hour before setting the flashy Z down for a superb landing. Six thousand people were on hand, all wanting to greet them at the same time as the crowding newsmen. Auto horn blasts and drum and bugle corps helped create pandemonium. It was sure great to be rich, famous and back in the old home town. Bayles was interviewed by the press and had the following comment: "The air was perfect, my ship was very stable and behaved well in the turns. The engine performed beautifully and the race was a great deal of fun." It sounds a

Bob Hall, chief designer for the Granvilles in 1931, smiles happily from the *City of Springfield* cockpit after winning the General Tire and Rubber Trophy.
United States Air Force

little corny now but they ate it up. The celebration continued with an afternoon parade, fireworks at night and, of course, culminated with that well-known American institution, the testimonial roast beef and peas dinner. Meanwhile, the Z and its Gee Bee companions were roped off on the flying field and lighted with floodlights well into the night so that everybody could get a look at these fabulous creations.

At the testimonial dinner, Bayles was a man of few words. "Last year at a dinner of welcome (after his Derby victory) I forgot the last half of my speech. This year, I am going to give the last half first. Bob Hall gave me the chance to fly *The City of Springfield*. Grannie gave Bob his chance to design the plane, the Tait brothers made it possible for Grannie to bring his force of workers together and to them should go a large share of the credit for our success at Cleveland. Now I find I have forgotten the first half of my speech. Thank you."

Zantford Granville then gave a brief introduction of his brothers and other personnel from the Granville Aircraft organization. He lauded them for their untiring efforts—working all night at times, the occasional lack of paychecks—and congratulated them for the now successful completion of their jobs.

Benny Howard's *Pete* flew against the Model Z in the 1931 Thompson, coming in sixth at 163.6 miles per hour.

Bob Hall spoke briefly about his feelings when he first flew the Z, and he also recounted his dismay when he tore up the wing tip of the Y on a tree top in Cleveland during the Nationals. Maude Tait said a few modest words about herself

making "an honest-to-Pete record." Some of the stockholders passed the hat and chipped in a share of their profits to Hall and Bayles, sort of a thank you for a fine job!

With the party now over, it was time to get down to business with the next step. The next big race would not be until 1932, but there was still the world's speed record to break. Bayles had originally wanted to do this at Cleveland where the F.A.I. course was set up, but fate had stepped in with two Granville employees being hurt in a motorcycle accident near Ashtabula, Ohio, while on their way back from the races to Springfield. Grannie had flown over from Cleveland to make temporary hospital arrangements, then Bayles flew them home in a Ford Trimotor. By the time these duties were completed, it was too late for the speed record attempt at Cleveland. For the moment, then, nothing could be done until suitable arrangements could be made for timing the runs over a measured course under F.A.I. rules. The only activity the Z saw during this period was to be displayed at the Eastern States Exhibition in Springfield that fall. Finally, arrangements were made with officials to set up for the attempt at the Wayne County Airport near Detroit.

Bayles picked up the Z from the Pratt and Whitney plant on November 6, where a new 750 horsepower Wasp Sr. engine had been installed along with a new, much larger cowl to accommodate it. This constituted a power increase of about thirty percent over the previously fitted Wasp Jr. If shear, raw power could do the job, this plane now had it. The current official

Lowell Bayles and the Gee Bee Z teamed up to win the 1931 Thompson Trophy Race at 236.239 miles per hour.
Thompson Products

land speed record was quite old, having been set by a Frenchman, Florintin Bonnet, flying a Bernard V–2 on December 11, 1924. It stood at 278.48 miles per hour and had been measured over an official F.A.I. three-kilometer (1.8642 mile) course. Bayles set out at once for the Curtiss plant at Buffalo, New York, to have a larger propeller fitted to the massive engine to better absorb the high horsepower output. Meanwhile, Grannie and Maude Tait decided that as long as the course was set up, she might as well try for the women's world speed record in the Y.

During late November and early December, Bayles made three attempts to surpass the record, but to no avail. On one pass he whipped through the traps at a sensational 314 miles per hour. Each time he had attempted to make the four required passes, either the propeller or the engine became troublesome enough to negate the high-speed tries. Maude Tait, with troubles of her own, finally had to give up her attempt and return to Springfield. She was about to become Mrs. James Moriarty.

The first of a long line of tragedies struck the high flying Gee Bee organization: Bayles was killed. During his third record attempt, the week before, he had averaged 282 miles per hour. However, his first pass fell victim to timing camera failure, and the record was unofficial. Now, on December 5, at about 1:00 P.M., Bayles had climbed the powerful Z out of the Wayne County Airport to about 1,000 feet and a point five miles from the course. He then banked around into a shallow dive toward the course, gaining maximum velocity as he hit the traps.

The Z rests between record attempts in a Detroit–Wayne County Airport hangar, a picture of brute power.

C. Mandrake

Suddenly, the Z heaved upward. The automotive-style gas cap had come loose and demolished the windscreen with terrible force. It hit Bayles in the face, shattering his goggles and knocking them loose into the slipstream. His half-conscious reflex actions threw the Z into a climb and then a vicious snap roll. With that, a wing came off under the extreme stress imposed by the maneuver that caused the craft to roll even faster until impact. The Z disintegrated into fifty yards of rubble along a railroad track. The Pratt and Whitney broke loose and rolled 200 yards from the wreckage. Bayles, of course, was killed instantly, spared the last few seconds by being knocked unconscious by the windscreen explosion. His body lay fifty feet from the wreck in a road that paralleled the railroad tracks. While there was much speculation that high-speed flutter had caused the wing to rip off, Grannie was given Bayles' goggles and parts of the broken windscreen that were found by some kids along the Z flight path well before the point of impact. This, of course, indicated the accident had occurred in the air preceding the tragic crash. Being so short coupled, the drastic pullup had placed more G's on the wing than it was ever designed for. For years afterwards, films of this crash were dubbed in whenever a dramatic air crash scene was needed in the movies. A worse tragedy could not have happened to the people of Springfield, nor the country for that matter. Bayles was a national hero. In a brief period of two years, he had become one of the foremost pilots of the day and had accepted the mantle of hero worship

Lowell Bayles and the Z at Detroit for world speed record attempt. Aircraft was powered by a massive 750 horsepower Pratt and Whitney Wasp Sr. engine.

T. C. Weaver Collection

This photo, while foggy, is interesting because it shows the massive size of the engine in contrast to the man and aircraft behind it. One pass during the record attempt was 314 miles per hour.

Goreing Collection

with such calm grace that he was endeared to all who knew him. Deep gloom pervaded the Granville organization. Grannie, who thought of Bayles as closely as any of his brothers, was devastated. He took Bayles's body back to the young flyer's Illinois home town for the funeral. The thought of building another racing aircraft was repugnant to him.

About this time, two other aircraft were completed and emerged from the Granville shop. One was built in just a week, to keep the troops exercised. It was a tail-first, or canard, design with the wing and tail taken from a derelict Aeronca. Emerging on November 26, it had a span of thirty-eight feet, a length of sixteen feet and was propelled by a twenty-eight-horsepower Aeronca engine. The *Ascender*, as it was called, heralded the same pun that was to develop with the Curtiss XP–35 canard design years later during World War II. The first flight was on December 1 and it was flown a few times afterwards before being scrapped. One of the last tasks of Bob Hall at the Granvilles' was to fly to New York to pick up a cylinder for the little rearward-flying beast. He then went with the Baltron Flying School. This was only a few days before the Bayles crash. Bayles's death, of course, far overshadowed Hall's resignation as far as Granville Aircraft was concerned.

The second craft that came from the shop was a singular example of Ed Granville's, who had designed and built a small single-seater all his own. The result was to once more show the abilities of the brothers in aircraft design and construction. It was nose-heavy but it flew, and he called it the *Tiger*.

A movement meanwhile began in Springfield to commemorate Bayles with the Lowell Bayles Memorial Flying Trophy. It would be awarded at the 1932 Nationals which were once again to be held at Cleveland.

Gee Bee
R-1 SUPER SPORTSTER

NR2100
manufactured by
Granville Bros. Aircraft
Springfield, Mass.

Mendenhall

Engine Cowl and Boots by
HILL AIRCRAFT STREAMLINERS

Goodrich Tires
AIRCRAFT PRODUCTS CO.
Greases and Oils

FIRST FLIGHT CONFIGURATION: AUGUST 13, 1932   TEST PILOT: RUSSELL BOARDMAN

3

R-1: Super Sportster

BOLD AND RADICAL in concept, the Gee Bee R-1 racer was built with but one thing in mind: to go like the hammers of hell! The R-1's lineage was pure enough. It was preceded by the race-winning Models X, Y and Z. The prestigious Z, of course, was the 1931 Thompson Trophy winner, *City of Springfield*. The craft was only marginally stable longitudinally, which many racing pilots of that era preferred over a 'stiff' aircraft. If you could handle her, she was maneuverable, to say the least, and that was how air races were won. However, the 1932 R-1 pilot, Jimmy Doolittle, usually calm and collected, but now sweat-drenched from the rigors of the race, was asked how she flew. "Don't ask me," he reportedly exclaimed, "I never did *fly* that wild son of a bitch!" That was in September 1932. The radical R-1 was destined to reach the heights and the depths of air racing in the early 1930's.

In January 1932 the Granville organization was in trouble. Its chief engineer, Bob Hall, had left in anger and frustration; his classic design, the Model Z, had crashed; its pilot, Lowell Bayles, was killed. In nine months the Thompson was coming up again, so without the Z it would be necessary to build a new racer even better than the fleet Z. Russell Boardman had bought up fifty-one percent of S.A.R.A. stock and was ready to bankroll a new racing campaign.

One of the first steps was to acquire a new degree-holding chief engineer to fill Bob Hall's shoes. This turned out to be a quiet, modest young man who had graduated from New York University, specifically the well-known Guggenheim School of Aeronautics. His name was Howell 'Pete' Miller. Not only was he formally educated in aeronautical technology, but he was experienced. He had served stints at both Huff Daland and at the Keystone bomber plant. Miller apparently sized Grannie up for what he was, a diamond in the rough. Grannie needed him for formal back-up. With no real technical training in stress analysis calculations or aerodynamic theory, Grannie could not build the far-out designs he could envision. Don DeLackner and Allen Morse also joined the Granville engineering staff shortly thereafter.

Meanwhile, Gee Bee racing was still going on. At the January 1932 Miami Air Races, C. A. Nott had won the Cuban Trophy, a closed-course race. He took it at 132.583 miles per hour in a Gee Bee Sportster. Nott then spent five weeks touring the southland at airshows, further telling the gospel of speed according to Granville. Unfortunately, on his return to Springfield, he upended the Sportster during landing. His only injury was his pride.

An 800 horsepower Wasp Sr. was obtained on loan from Pratt and Whitney, and it was decided to keep the craft short-coupled to cut wetted area, along with using minimal wings, similar to the Model Z. The pilot would, by necessity, be seated far back to balance the engine.

The teardrop was in fashion in those days of aerodynamic science as the most streamlined shape possible. In a way, it made some sense, because a free-falling drop of water forms into a teardrop shape, offering the least possible air resistance. Therefore, put that big Pratt and Whitney radial up front and start fairing a teardrop shape from it even though the already large fuselage grew still greater in girth back of the engine. Though large, it was still the most theoretically perfect streamlined shape. That's the direction they took.

While they were at it, they would also build a sister ship with a smaller 550 horsepower Wasp Jr. engine and a larger fuel tank for range, and take the Bendix, too! The Thompson racer would be the R-1, the Bendix sister ship would be the R-2. Just to make sure they were not going off on a wild tangent, Grannie and Howell Miller took a model of the new aircraft to New York University for some wind tunnel work. Alexander Klemin, Miller's professor while at NYU, aided in the tests. Finally, Grannie and Miller agreed they were satisfied to go ahead with the project. The tests confirmed that the teardrop shape was of maximum streamlining for the anticipated speed range of the new aircraft.

A close look at the subsequently designed structure and its features reveals the design details to be somewhat unremarkable and soundly, even conservatively, engineered. It was when these parts were assembled into a whole that the radical aircraft appeared.

A walk around the R-1 as it left the Granville shop would have disclosed the following trim, appointments and construction: The traditional Gee Bee scalloped paint scheme was extra-brilliant and glossy red and white with a black pinstripe separating the colors. It was obtained with fourteen hand-rubbed coats of Titanine dope. The shape of the cavernous fuselage expanded outward to a true sixty-one-inch-diameter circle at a point about one-third the length back from the nose. The rudder, over a foot thick at the hinge line, tapered to a sharp edge at the rear of the craft and, in its original configuration, had no vertical fin. Grannie was unsure about just how much fin area was needed and decided to wait until after the first test flight to add more area if it appeared to be required. The fuselage cross-section between the sixty-one-inch true circle and the rudder was one of gradually increasing elipses.

The big, hopped-up 1,334-cubic-inch nine-cylinder radial Pratt and Whitney delivered 800 horsepower at 2,350 revolutions per minute. It had a 6:1 compression ratio and a 12:1 super-charger ratio. There was no exhaust manifold as the stub stacks were designed to blend the hot exhaust gas in with the cooling air as it exited from under the cowl. A Smith controllable-pitch propeller was used to allow rapid acceleration at takeoff. The bulbous engine cowling had a ½-inch steel tube ring rolled into its leading edge. It was fabricated for Granville Brothers by Hill Aircraft Streamliners. Constructed of hammered alumi-num, it was firmly fastened by a series of turnbuckles and brace rods to both the engine and fuselage to prevent its being pulled forward into the prop at high speeds. Behind the firewall was a 160-gallon fuel tank and an eighteen-gallon oil tank. The filler caps for these were located inside the fuselage—the Z's crash cause was well remembered.

The fuselage structure was typical of the previous Models X, Y and Z. A strong welded structure of chrome molybdenum steel tubing, strengthened by traverse diagonal bracing, formed the central framework. Wing mounts and landing gear strut bracing were an integral part of the welded tube frame. Plywood was used for the formers, floor and seat back. The aft section was fabric covered over spruce stringers. The forward fuselage and the area around the cockpit was covered with aluminum sheeting. Additional fuselage features of this seventeen-foot nine-inch long aircraft were retractable handles near the tail for easy ground handling, plus a hard point for resting the rear fuselage on a sawhorse, enabling easy access for engine main-tenance.

The cockpit featured a polished red leather seat that was easy to slide off of for quick bailouts. It was equipped with a full complement of flight and navigation instruments including an Elgin tachometer, airspeed indicator, altimeter, compass and thermometer. The oil pressure gauge and other instruments were manufactured by Pioneer. The windscreen was fashioned of three pieces of Indestructo shatterproof safety glass. Fiberloid was chosen for the canopy. The assembly was joined together with riveted aluminum framing. It was designed to give right-angle undistorted vision to the pilot and, in an emergency, the assembly could be released quickly with inside levers. Small cleaning hand-holes were on either side near the windscreen panes.

Entry to the cockpit was through a door on the craft's star-board side. The door featured quick-disconnect hinges to allow getting it off rapidly in case of an emergency bailout. Venti-lation for the cockpit was achieved by means of two large rubber tubes running from between the engine cylinders rearward to either side of the cockpit. Temperature was controlled by a system of dampers. The stick was held in the right hand with throttle and propeller controls operated by the left. A small

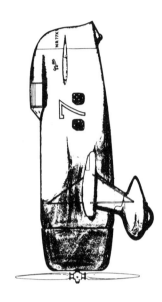

Gee Bee
SUPER-SPORTSTER

SPECIFICATIONS

ENGINE – PRATT & WHITNEY "WASP"
SPAN – 25 FT   GROSS WING AREA – 101.9 SQ.FT.
CHORD (ROOT) – 4 FT. 5 IN.   WHEEL-TREAD – 76 IN.

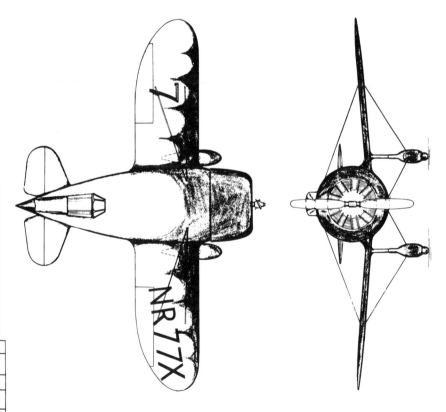

NR77X

THREE-VIEW SUPER-SPORTSTER

GRANVILLE BROTHERS AIRCRAFT, INC.
SPRINGFIELD, MASS.

hand-wheel was also located on the left side for elevator trim.

As mentioned before, the landing gear was anchored to steel tubing structures that were integral with the main fuselage frame. The heart of the gear was a Cleveland Pneumatic Tool Company Aerol air-and-oil shock absorber with a five-inch travel. Aircraft Products wheels and Warner mechanical brakes, which were actuated by pulling the stick all the way back and then applying the brake pedals, were mounted in the two forked, articulated assemblies. Tires were Goodrich 6 x 10's with twenty-three-inch diameter. Hammered aluminum wheel pants, also by Hill Aircraft Streamliners, rode up and down with the wheels giving maximum streamlining to the gear at all times. Fully extended, the distance from the ground to propeller centerline was 63.5 inches. The wheel tread was a narrow seventy-six inches, not much of a deterrent to ground looping. The tail wheel was a sponge rubber tire on an aluminum hub. This was mounted on a three-inch-travel oleo strut—the whole assembly moving with the rudder. On the ground, the rudder connection could be unlatched, allowing the tail wheel to be full-castoring for easier handling.

The twenty-five-foot-span wings mounted to the integral fuselage wing stubs were supported by streamlined Stewart-Hartshorn landing and flying wires—two above, two below. This wire was also used for cross-bracing between the two landing gear struts. The airfoil section was a modified M–6, being slightly thinner than the parent airfoil. The wing was of constant fifty-three-inch chord and thickness to a point outboard eighty-eight inches from the fuselage centerline. The structure was two spruce spars with ribs made of Haskelite plywood spaced on five-inch centers throughout the whole span. Areas of high stress were reinforced with aluminum plates and wire cross-bracing. The entire framework was covered with plywood and, finally, doped fabric. The result was a true airfoil shape over the entire span of the wing, as opposed to fabric-covered wings where the fabric shrinks and sags between the ribs. This feature produced more efficient lift for the whole wing—and the R–1 would use all the lift it could muster. Wings were rigged to the fuselage with a 2.5-degree angle of incidence and 4.5-degree dihedral. The wing-to-fuselage juncture was nicely covered with large, hammered aluminum fillets, riveted in place. Wing loading was 24.15 pounds per square foot at racing gross; 30.75 pounds per square foot with a full tank.

The control surfaces operated in an entirely conventional manner, except they were far stronger than usual to overcome any flutter tendency at high speeds. The rudder, the top of which was, at first, flush with the canopy, was actuated by the normal cable-horn method.

The stabilizer was built up similarly to the wing: two spruce spars, Haskelite plywood ribs and covering. It was stressed to take a seventy-five pound per square foot loading, with a one hundred percent safety factor over this figure in highly stressed areas. It was hinged at the front spar with a fifteen-degree travel

Prepared by Howell Miller in July 1932, this general arrangement drawing showed a startled aviation world the type of aircraft the Granville organization was building for that year's Nationals.

Granville Brothers Aircraft

adjustment available to the pilot. As it moved up and down, a two-inch constant-radius fillet, spring attached to the fuselage, moved with it. This adjustment, as described before, was cable controlled by a wheel on the left side of the cockpit. The elevators worked by means of a push/pull rod plus a cable backup system attached to the control stick.

The statically balanced ailerons were of the torque tube variety with the trailing edge and formed sheet steel ribs welded to the torque tube. The hinges were ball bearings. Angular ball and sockets were used for all torque tube joints. This type of construction eliminated the danger of flutter with a subsequent disaster of the ailerons pulling off the wing at high speed. Racing gross weight of the R-1 was 2,415 pounds with fifty gallons in the tank. With a full tank, gross weight rose to 3,025 pounds. Empty weight was 1,840 pounds.

A test flight of a new aircraft, particularly one as radical as the R-1, in those days was a hairy adventure. Unlike today's

The Gee Bee R-1 in spite of its hefty girth was beautifully streamlined, as shown in this three-quarter rear view.

Paramount Studios–Springfield

crisply scientific and usually predictable first flights, the pilot did not have hours of flight time in a simulator behind him. In the case of the R-1, Russell Boardman, manager of S.A.R.A., elected to make the first flight. He had become interested in air racing after setting an international distance record to Turkey with Johnnie Polando. In the Spring of 1932 he had flown Maude Tait's Model Y in the Omaha Air Races. He won the feature race, a free-for-all, at 182.36 mph. The following day, he won the Charles 'Speed' Holman Aerobatic Trophy. He had recently returned to Springfield to help raise money for the Lowell Bayles Memorial Trophy by putting on aerobatic displays for the hometown fans.

On the evening of August 10, George Agnoli, the painter, put the final touches on the R-1 and probably heaved a great sigh of relief after applying the fourteenth coat of dope. The National Air Races were scheduled for August 27 through September 10. Not much time was left. On Friday, August 12, the R-1 rolled out and engine adjustments were made. Word got around that it was about to fly and several thousand people converged on the airport to watch. The Granvilles had released a side view of the aircraft to the newspapers a week earlier. People had made dire predictions for this radical, finless flying engine. In fact, a riddle made the rounds: "What is more dangerous than going over Niagara Falls in a barrel?" The answer, "Flying one!" Unfortunately, more work was required during the day on the powerplant and this went on till 11:00 P.M. that night.

On the thirteenth, the R-1 was out again at 5:00 A.M. The Wasp was run in for about forty-five minutes to smooth out any roughness. A gas leak developed due to a faulty fuel pump, and for a few moments there was even a danger of fire. However, by 9:00 A.M. all seemed well. Boardman strapped on his chute and posed beside the R-1 for the press before entering the cockpit through the side door. As he opened up the Pratt and Whitney, the grass flattened in the prop wash behind the R-1, and bits of dirt and debris forced the spectators to shield their eyes. The craft slowly trundled away to the far side of the field. The spectators held their breath as, with a bit more throttle, it turned its massive red cowl into the wind. The aircraft sat for a few minutes, the polished propeller ticking over and throwing highlighted reflections back at the distant crowd. Soon, across the field, the throaty roar of the big Wasp reverberated as Boardman brought up the power and the ship began to move. Faster and faster, with tail up, it skipped across the grass until it seemed about to leave the ground. Boardman then cut the throttle and slowed to a stop. He swung the ship around and returned to his starting point. Again, the engine's powerful roar increased as the ship gathered speed rapidly. The Smith controllable-pitch prop bit deeply into the morning air and this time the wheels left the ground. Boardman began a long, slow climb out over the power lines, heading across the river for Bowles Agawam Field.

The spectators quickly took to their cars to pursue the craft. They wanted to be on hand for the landing—if there was one. At Bowles Agawam, Bob Hall waited with some of his people who manned emergency equipment should it be needed. Though no longer with the Granvilles, it was a case of the fraternity of airmen looking out for each other when the going might get rough. Boardman, in the air, had quickly accelerated to an air speed of 240 miles per hour without even trying—300 miles per hour should be a cinch. One thing, though, without a fin, the damned thing fishtailed badly due to a lack of directional stability. One false move and the end would arrive promptly! This would have to be fixed to make the craft suitable for racing. Arriving at Bowles Agawam, about a half-hour after takeoff, Boardman neatly set the big Gee Bee down amid the cheers of a gathering crowd. "You boys sure build airplanes," he reportedly exclaimed to the waiting Granvilles.

That night, they put the R-1 on a flatbed truck and hauled her back to the Granville factory. Two square feet of fin and rudder were quickly designed and added to the fuselage behind the cockpit to correct the fishtailing problem.

Bob Hall, during this period, was still very much on the air racing scene. Though he had left the Granville Brothers, he was still a first-class race plane designer and had decided to strike out on his own in that field. He had founded a new company, Springfield Aircraft, Incorporated, at Bowles Agawam Field. To start with, he had two firm orders for racing aircraft,

This full-front view of the R-1 emphasizes the large 61-inch fuselage diameter needed to house the 800 horsepower Pratt and Whitney Wasp Sr.
Pratt and Whitney

certainly based on his earlier success as the designer of the Z, *City of Springfield*.

The first order was from well-to-do sportsman, Frank Lynch. The plane was somewhat larger than the usual racer and of high gull-winged design. Lynch wanted it for a round-the-world speed flight, hence it was fitted with a staggered side-by-side seating configuration for two people. It was christened the *Cicada*, a large Mexican moth or locust, and painted accordingly with green, cream and brown designs on its fuselage and wings to resemble that insect. The insect's eyes were painted on either side of the cowl. After its first flight in the early evening of June twenty-fourth when the air was calm, midnight oil was burned by Hall and his workers to make some last-minute fixes. The next morning, he was off early for the honeymooners' paradise, Niagara Falls, for the last day of that city's International Air Races. In the final event, the Niagara Falls Manufacturers Trophy Race, Hall flew the *Cicada* to fourth place in the unlimited free-for-all—not too bad for a ship designed specifically for distance racing instead of pylon racing.

After returning to Springfield with the *Cicada*, the final touches were added before delivery to Lynch. Lynch thought he might run it in the 1932 Bendix Trophy Race, but engine problems precluded that.

The second plane that Hall had contracted to build sat nearly completed in the hangar of Bowles Agawam when Boardman landed the big R–1 after its first flight. This red and black (with

The big red and white R-1, race number 11, gets an engine runup at the 1932 Nationals. Ship at racing gross weighed 2,415 pounds.

United States Air Force

a white pinstripe) gull-winged beauty was a single-place racer designed to win the upcoming Thompson in direct competition with the Gee Bee R–1. The race number assigned for Cleveland was 6 and the license number was NR–2111. Marion Price Guggenheim, of the New York family noted for their financial support of the aeronautical world, had contracted for it to be raced by Russell Thaw. Thaw was chief pilot of the family's Lockheed Vega and Air Express. The Yale University mascot was the namesake of the new craft. It was named *Bulldog.*

While Hall chose a gull-wing design, the plane was still endowed with the stubbiness of his earlier Z. In fact, if you were to put the gull wings on the earlier fuselage of the Z, you would essentially have the *Bulldog.*

Particulars of the Hall *Bulldog* were as follows: Fuselage construction was similar to its Gee Bee predecessors with welded steel tube framework, wood formers and stringers and fabric covering. The fuselage length was nineteen feet, and its forward portions and around the cockpit were covered with sheet aluminum. The wing and tail assemblies were wood with fabric covering, except for the aluminum-covered fin. A quick-release canopy, very similar to the Model Z, was fitted. The twenty-six-foot wing span, gull-winged as it was, was supported by fairly massive 'V' struts on either wing. The powerplant was a Pratt and Whitney Wasp Jr. 985 rated at 535 horsepower, driving a model-shop hand-made Hamilton Standard controllable-pitch propeller. The end result was 243.7-miles-per-hour top speed. Hall had chosen the gull wing because, in his opinion, it would improve longitudinal stability—something lacking in the Gee Bee designs he had been exposed to thus far. An interesting exhaust system had outlets at right angles to the cowl to better scavenge the exhaust gases. This was expected to increase the volumetric efficiency of the supercharger.

Testing began in early August. On his first trial flight, the *Bulldog* rolled sharply left at about ten feet after takeoff. Hall cut the engine, regained control and rolled out straight ahead. A tire was blown and the left wheel pant was damaged. It was evident more fin and rudder were needed to counteract the extreme torque of the Pratt and Whitney on such a small, short-coupled aircraft. The rudder was changed four times, the fin three times, before the flying characteristics were judged satisfactory for the racing circuit. The gull wing, graceful and beautiful as it was, proved to be aerodynamically disappointing and a great deal different than Hall had calculated and anticipated. At the same time, the exotic exhaust system seemed to create more problems than it solved. Since time was running out, it was scrapped. The expansion and contraction of its parts were normal phenomena but their adjustment would require more time than was available. Now, adding urgency, the Gee Bee R–1 piloted by Boardman had arrived at Bowles Agawam in full color and flourish.

The R–1 was parked in a corner of the same hangar where Hall was putting the finishing touches on the gull-winged

Bulldog. The big Gee Bee was hitting 275 miles per hour easily during flight tests. All seemed to be progressing well toward the showdown at Cleveland when fate beckoned. Boardman crashed in a Model E Sportster while flying over to Bowles Agawam for some fine tuning of the R–1. He had taken off, spun left, recovered, spun right, then with a bone-shaking thump he crashed into some woods near the field. When extracted from the wreckage, he was conscious but needed hospitalization. For a while he felt he would recover enough to fly the R–1 at Cleveland, but finally he grudgingly realized that was impossible. So, two weeks before the race, the R–1 and its Bendix sister ship, the R–2, were complete and ready to go—but without pilots.

Hundreds of miles away in Wichita, Kansas, on August 23, Jimmy Doolittle was testing his highly modified Laird Super Solution biplane. The aircraft had been redesigned from the year before (when it won the Bendix), with the massive wheel pants replaced by a retractable landing gear that folded upward and inward into the fuselage bottom. The canopy and cockpit area were completely revised for better visibility and the ship was repainted Shell red and yellow replete with the company's seashell trademark.

He had completed about twenty minutes of refamiliarization with the pert, little speedster and now prepared to land. He found the new retractable gear would not extend completely. After trying to cycle it to no avail, he dropped a note to the ground crew watching below: "Something is wrong with landing gear. Can get 3½ turns each way. If any suggestions, write on side of plane and come up. Otherwise, I will run out of gas and stall in." Soon another aircraft joined him.

On its side was the instructive message in bold letters: "ZOOM RIGHT, ZOOM LEFT, POWER DIVE." Immediately Jimmy threw the little craft violently into the prescribed maneuvers. After ten minutes of this, the landing gear was still firmly in place. It was evident Doolittle had but two choices: bail out, or bring the Super Solution in for a wheels-up landing. For a man like Doolittle, that was not really a choice. He would save the plane, bringing her in with the least amount of damage possible. Perhaps it would be minor enough that the aircraft could still be repaired for the next week's Thompson. Jimmy flew around for nearly another two hours waiting for the fuel to burn off, then began his descent to the grassy part of the field below. Master pilot that he was, the Super Solution was held off till the last possible amount of airspeed had been drained off. The prop bit into the turf as Jimmy cut the switches. About the same time, the semi-retracted gear made contact with a shuddering crunch. The plane slithered along the grass and finally came to a stop. Damage to the fuselage bottom was minor. Jimmy unbuckled and swung out of the cockpit to examine his pranged speedster. It was repairable but the damage was still too great to mend in time for the following week's Nationals at Cleveland.

News travels fast and the wire services quickly picked up the story. Indeed, photographers had been present and recorded Jimmy standing beside the crippled craft right after the mishap. The partnership between one of the greatest flyers of all time and the most famous racing plane of all time occurred during a telephone call on August 27 between Doolittle and Zantford Granville. Grannie asked Jimmy if he would like to fly the R-1 in the upcoming Shell Speed Dashes and, of course, the Thompson Trophy Race. "Yes," answered Jimmy, getting right to the point. It was agreed that Jimmy would fly to Springfield in the Shell Lockheed Vega and arrive the next day, a Sunday.

Word traveled fast around town and he was met by several hundred race fans as he taxied the big Vega up to the hangar at Bowles Agawam. He got out of the aircraft, paying little attention to the crowd, and walked straight over to the gleaming

Bob Hall's *Springfield Bulldog* **was as radical in appearance as its Gee Bee opponents. Painted red and black, the aircraft was disappointing on the race course.**

W. F. Yeager

R–1 standing in the sunshine. Grannie and his brothers and co-workers were waiting for him. Doolittle thought of this little bomb's immediate ancestor, the also short-coupled Model Z, *City of Springfield*. He had seen the newsreels of Bayles's fiery crash in December of the previous year at Detroit. Still, if he was to win the Thompson, this was the only ship to do it in. He pushed the previous year's tragedy from his mind and began examining the big radial-engined speed merchant.

The crowd watched him from a distance, for he was somewhat of a national hero because of his 1925 Schneider Trophy victory and his world's first blind instrument landing for Sperry Gyroscope in 1929. He also had attended many air shows and races around the country in his Shell-sponsored Travel Air Model R and Laird Solution airplanes. He had, in addition, completed his doctorate in aeronautical engineering (Phi Beta Kappa) at Massachusetts Institute of Technology during the late 1920's. He was the school's first graduate of this program. No backyard mechanic or seat-of-the-pants flyer was this gentleman. Later, of course, as an Army Air Corps general, he became a World War II legend for leading the morale-building 1942 B–25 raid on Tokyo off the carrier *Hornet*.

As he examined the aircraft, one wag's statement came to mind: "The aircraft has no center of gravity." One of the Granville brothers used a screwdriver to open the cockpit door, far aft on the fuselage side. It was very apparent that from this position the visibility on the ground was practically nonexistent over and around the big red cowl.

While inspecting, he kept up a rapid-fire barrage of questions to Grannie and others until he was finally satisfied with the answers. The pact for greatness was sealed. The airfield had not been used a great deal that season and the late summer grass was long and specked colorfully with bluebells and Queen Anne's Lace waving in the sunny afternoon breeze.

The first flight of Doolittle in the speedy juggernaut was prepared for with several Granville people pushing the R–1 across the field for about half a mile to its takeoff position. Jimmy took a last walk around as large chocks were pushed under the wheels preparatory to engine startup. Doolittle climbed in the open side door. The door was carefully pushed closed and latched behind him. As he buckled up, it began to grow warm beneath the greenhouse pyralin canopy. Someone asked Jimmy where he was going for the first flight. Doolittle answered evenly from deep within the R–1, "Cleveland, of course." Interviewed later by reporters, he said, "Since I hadn't flown the plane before, it made little difference whether the hop was a long one or a short one." The big Smith controllable prop began slowly to turn and, as Doolittle primed, several of the cylinders caught and rumbled as blue-white oil smoke billowed from the exhaust stacks. In a couple of seconds, the ragged coughing flared into the powerful unique roar of the Pratt and Whitney Wasp—all nine cylinders in song. The

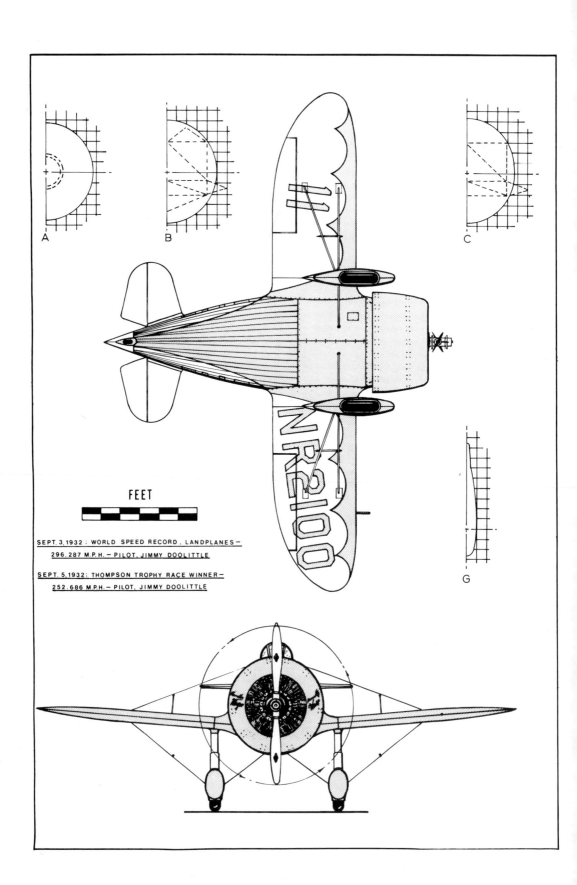

A

B

C

G

FEET

SEPT. 3, 1932 : WORLD SPEED RECORD, LANDPLANES—
296.287 M.P.H. — PILOT, JIMMY DOOLITTLE

SEPT. 5, 1932: THOMPSON TROPHY RACE WINNER—
252.686 M.P.H. — PILOT, JIMMY DOOLITTLE

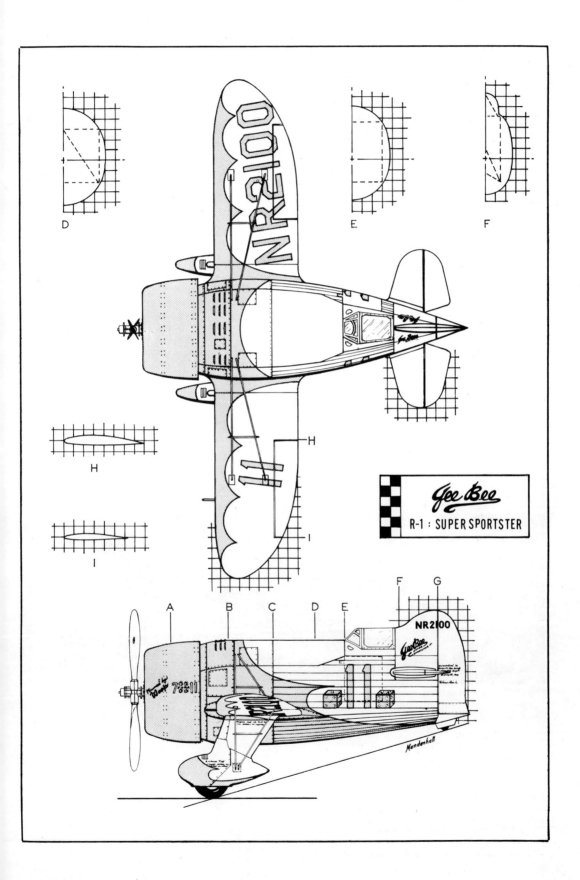

D

E

F

H

I

Gee Bee

R-1 : SUPER SPORTSTER

NR2100

A B C D E F G

H

I

Mendenhall

propeller was now a shimmering silver disc in the strong sunlight. As the engine warmed up, Jimmy advanced the throttle to full power, the exhaust barely visible. Crewmen hung onto the wing tips and the wheels pushed hard against the chocks. Gravel, dirt and bluebells flew in a plume behind the howling propwash. Jimmy then throttled back and signaled the crew to release the wing tips and remove the chocks. He was now ready to roll.

Taking a last deep breath, he opened the throttle evenly, letting the speed build until he could feel the bite of the rudder in the airstream, then opened on up to full power. The controllable-pitch prop in fine pitch was biting up huge chunks of air as it was whirled at full throttle. Jimmy lifted the tail only a few inches as the hurtling machine cut a swath through the hayfield. Inside, as the wheel rumbling stopped, Jimmy carefully gained altitude and gradually edged the big nose ahead of him onto a course toward Cleveland. Almost immediately, he confirmed in his own mind that he had one hot airplane

Ready for racing, the R-1 sits pert and attentive at the flight line.

T. C. Weaver Collection

on his hands. It would demand a pilot's continual attention. He later said, "It was the trickiest plane I have ever been in. Flying it was like balancing a pencil on the tip of your finger." On the ground, the Granvilles and the spectators watched their progeny disappear into the western sky with the throaty roar of the Pratt and Whitney now like the gentle buzz of a bee. Soon both the sound and the dot in the sky disappeared and a kind of awed silence pervaded the airfield. As people filed back to their cars, some muttered that Doolittle did exactly what he wanted to do. He didn't even circle the field before he left.

In the R–1, Jimmy could see the Hudson River coming up and the hills of New York state ahead. Occasionally he nudged the stick one way or the other, carefully but firmly coordinating the rudder pedals to get the feel of this powerful beast which he would soon be racing in the greatest air race of all time— the 1932 Thompson. Two hours later, Grannie received a telegram: "Landed O.K. Cleveland."

The R–2, except for the smaller engine cowl, had the same lines as the R–1. T. C. Weaver Collection

Gee Bee

R-1 SUPER SPORTSTER

NR2100

Mendenhall

INBOARD PROFILE

4

7–11 at the Races

CLEVELAND, CLEVELAND BESET with problems—
pollution to the point the Cuyahoga River once caught fire!
It was also the first major American city to go bankrupt—but
it wasn't always that way. In 1932 it was Mecca for the speed
merchants.

In 1929, at Cleveland, Doug Davis trounced the Army and
Navy with his Travel Air Mystery Ship in the Thompson Cup
Race. In 1930, the races were in Chicago but in 1931, Lowell
Bayles had flown the bombshell Gee Bee *City of Springfield*
to a sizzling victory at Cleveland. A tradition was established.

The 1932 races were to be held from August 27 through
September 5 and were viewed by race fans and press alike as
one bright spot in an otherwise gloomy economic period with
over twelve million people looking for work. Hall had left
Springfield for the upcoming races and the R–1 had been flown
in for the contest by Doolittle. Grannie took off for Cleveland
with the Model Y now powered by a new 450 horsepower Wasp.

One of the big events of the Cleveland Air Races was the
2,369-mile Bendix Trophy Race that originated in Los Angeles
and was a cross-country dash to Cleveland. Of course, the Gee
Bee ship, the R–2 number 7, was in Los Angeles for the start.
It was in most respects identical to Doolittle's R–1, except for
the smaller 550 horsepower Pratt and Whitney Wasp Jr. R–985.
Gross weight for this ship, however, was 3,885 pounds, versus
the R–1's 2,415 pounds. Most of this was attributed to the R–2's
larger-capacity fuel and oil tanks and their long-range contents.
Empty weight of the R–2 was actually less than that of the R–1—
1,796 pounds versus the latter's 1,840 pounds.

At the last minute on August 22, Lee Gehlbach, a former
Army pilot turned test pilot, had arrived at Springfield and was
offered the job of flying the R–2 in the Bendix. Others had
wanted that job but were not as well qualified as Gehlbach who
was noted for being highly skilled in flying fast airplanes. He
had no trouble with the R–2 number 7 ship, bringing it up to
the standards of the R–1 when he assumed the duties of test

pilot. He was assisted by A. M. Banks, another former Army pilot. During one test flight, a flying wire snapped with no problem noted except that it marred the paint on the fuselage sides where it slapped in the slipstream. Fifty degrees above normal oil temperatures was an area of concern; however, no real reason could be found. Finally, Gehlbach took off for Los Angeles on the twenty-fourth. Mark and Ed Granville were flown to Los Angeles and Kansas City respectively to watch over the maintenance and refueling of the big number 7 entry as it made its way back across the country from United Airport in Burbank. Lee Gehlbach told newsmen he had "loafed along at speeds over 200 miles per hour" on his way to the West Coast from Springfield.

Since Jimmy Doolittle's flat-out speed to win the Bendix the previous year was only 233 miles per hour, it meant for sure the Gee Bee R–2 was going to be a real contender in the upcoming race. Other pilots and aircraft entered in the race were Claire Vance and his twin-boom flying wing; along with three Wedell-Williams racers—Wedell himself in '44,' Jimmy Haizlip in '92'

Direct rear view of R-1 shows the fuselage getting greater in diameter behind the cowl, in line with the teardrop design philosophy used.

T. C. Weaver Collection

The most famous man/ machine team in the history of air racing: Jimmy Doolittle and the Gee Bee R-1.
T. C. Weaver Collection

and the colorful Roscoe Turner in his *Gilmore Special*. Other would-be entrants included Hall in the *Bulldog*, Lynch in the *Cicada*, and Doolittle in the Super Solution.

Russell Thaw had turned down the *Bulldog* at the last minute, saying the gull-winged aircraft just wasn't his idea of a racer. The aircraft was grounded while Hall scurried around to raise money to buy it back from the Guggenheims and race it at Cleveland himself. He managed to get the funds, but the Guggenheims refused to resell the *Bulldog* to Hall. Instead, they gave him permission to fly it. By this time it was too late for the Bendix. However, the Thompson at Cleveland still beckoned.

Doolittle, of course, was out of contention due to the forced landing of the Super Solution in Wichita the week before. Alexander de Seversky was considered to be a potential entrant with his new, all-metal monoplane, but it was not ready in time. Frank Lynch had thought of flying the *Cicada* in the Bendix as a sort of warmup for his around-the-world speed dash but gave up the idea after too much engine trouble. He was content to fly the *Cicada* to Cleveland, where it sat while he watched the races.

Soupy weather caused delay after delay in starting the Bendix race, but finally on August 29 the five starters got off the ground, the first plane taking off at 2:00 A.M. Because his plane was much larger and slower, Vance took off first (it had a fifty-five-foot wing span and carried 1,200 gallons of fuel in its ten fuel tanks). It was a veritable flying tank car. The dark blue craft was powered by a 535 horsepower Pratt and Whitney Wasp Jr. and could cruise at 185 miles per hour. Vance counted on a nonstop flight to Cleveland to make up for his lesser speed. At 3:30 A.M. Roscoe Turner roared into the air in his brand-new red and beige Wedell-Williams. By 3:45 A.M. the last three early birds, Haizlip, Wedell and Gehlbach, were also wrestling their heavy-with-fuel racers off the Burbank runway. Because of a lack of time for preparation, Vance soon found he had developed a leaky gas line and the stuff was starting to drip into the cockpit. He prudently banked around to an opposite heading and returned to Burbank—out of the race.

Haizlip's black and white Wedell headed for Goodland, Kansas, for a quick ten-minute, 140-gallon refueling stop. He had another 130-gallon stop in Lansing, Illinois, and then he was off to Cleveland. Gehlbach flew the R–2 to Amarillo, Texas, for a quick refuel, then headed northeast toward Cleveland. As he was climbing for altitude out of Amarillo, he noticed a few spots of oil on the windscreen. The spots soon grew in intensity as oil spurted from under the cowl. As he watched his oil pressure gauge drop, he knew he had a very bad leak somewhere up front. The small hand-openings for cleaning the windshield from inside the cockpit were inadequate to do the cleanup job that the rupture was causing. Flying blind, he set the R–2 down on Chanute Field at Rantoul, Illinois, hoping to fix the leak and refill his oil tank, which held twenty gallons. Once on the ground he found out it was a cracked oil line and it would be impossible to make repairs, so, topping off the oil, he again headed for Cleveland. He flew without the cockpit cover, which lowered his speed but allowed him to see. The cover, left at Chanute, was flown to Cleveland later so that the R–2 could compete in events there. When he arrived in Cleveland, the fuselage of the Gee Bee was streaked with oil

With the cockpit door off, the R-1 taxies into a left turn at Cleveland. The foot-thick rudder shows up well in this photo taken in front of the Skyways hangar.

C. Mandrake

its full length. Gehlbach himself was pretty much covered, too.

Jimmy Haizlip had arrived an hour and thirty minutes earlier, making him the Bendix winner of $6,750. Second place and $3,750 went to Jimmy Wedell. Turner was third for $2,250 and Gehlbach had to be content with $1,500—fourth-place money. Haizlip had not landed at Cleveland but continued on to New York's Floyd Bennett Field, à la Doolittle the previous year. He set a new transcontinental speed record of ten hours and nineteen minutes. He then returned to Cleveland for the races.

The events at Cleveland that year were the utmost in aerial pizzazz with Cliff Henderson, a controversial showman, as the impresario. Between races, such stunts as a blimp towing a glider with a lady parachutist jumping from the glider kept the show moving. The Lindbergh flight was a little over five years old and people still ran outside when an airplane droned over, so the Nationals were really something for them to see! Other attention-getters between racing events were a high hurdle race between two autogyros and a mock dog fight between a Curtiss Pusher and another autogyro. Of course, aerobatics, parachute jumping and deadstick landing contests were held. It was as gala as the state fair, complete with flags and cotton candy.

The military, while not competing, was there in force. The Marine Hell Divers were every bit as exciting as the Blue Angels or Thunderbirds are today, diving inverted in formation past

An interesting indoor shot of the R-1 in a Cleveland hangar. To its left can be seen one of the Keith Rider racers fitted with a then-new retract gear.

Strasser

the grandstands. There were eighteen P-6E's present along with a like number of P-16's, nine Curtiss Hell Divers, twenty-one P-12E's and four Keystone B-6's. That's seventy fighting craft—an air force in itself!

Foreign stunt pilots abounded, putting on exhibitions that were as daring as Art Scholl and Bob Hoover in today's air show circuit. For example, handsome, blonde Lieutenant Andrea Zotti of the Italian Air Force had an interesting little trick he performed. He climbed his Breda 19 straight up into the wind. Holding air speed just above stall speed he allowed the craft to drift backwards across the field in front of the stands.

Even death occurred before the crowds when the autogyro and Curtiss Pusher dog fight act was performed one day toward the end of the show. The autogyro was caught in a collision with the Pusher, killing the Curtiss pilot, Al Wilson. Aside from the heavy iron present (the Gee Bee R-1 and R-2, the three Wedell-Williams and the Hall *Bulldog*), there were myriad other racers for the lower-powered events. The Keith Rider San Francisco I and II Menasco-powered bombs were there. Art Chester's famous *Jeep* was not there (it was tied up with flight problems; Chester, therefore, was flying his Davis racer). John Livingston's Clipped Wing Monocoupe, Ray Liggett's Cessna, Wittman's *Chief Oshkosh* were present, as were the immortal Benny Howard with the white trio *Pete*, *Mike* and *Ike*, and Gordon Israel and his *Redhead*. Beside the above classics were literally hundreds of Curtiss Robins, Fairchilds, Stinsons, Wacos, Great

Doolittle and the R-1. *Time* magazine called them "a stubby sturdy pilot in a stubby sturdy ship."

Lakes, Travel Airs and Lairds, to name a few of many.

Since the beginning of the Nationals, the days had been generally cloudy with frequent showers, none of which, however, could possibly dampen the enthusiasm the air meet generated. Occasionally, the sun did peek through for a few hours.

During the early events, the Gee Bee name appeared among the contestants. William Rausch of White Plains, New York, flying a Menasco-powered Model E Sportster came in ninth in the William B. Leads Trophy Race—a sprint from New York's Roosevelt Field to Cleveland. Prize money for him was fifty dollars. He then flew the Sportster in the Division 2 Sohio Derby, taking seventh place and pocketing an additional twenty-five dollars in prize money. Surely the seventy-five dollars won didn't pay his expenses.

With the two super racers now in Cleveland along with their pilots Doolittle and Gehlbach, it was time to get down to the business of racing S.A.R.A.'s entries and making a few bucks. Jimmy Doolittle decided to get in a little practice on the Thompson Trophy course which was triangular in shape with the pylons ten miles apart. Jimmy took off still remembering the general touchiness of the R-1 on the flight from Springfield to Cleveland. Being a cautious pilot, there would be no grandstanding this trip for him. He climbed to 5,000 feet before setting the ship up on the race course below. Streaking along, he came over the first pylon and slammed the big, powerful R-1 into a tight knife-edge turn to see how she handled. She showed

The sister ship to the R-1 was the R-2, number 7. Powered by a smaller 550 horsepower Pratt and Whitney Wasp Jr., the ship was built for the cross-country Bendix Trophy Race.

T. C. Weaver Collection

With the engine fired up, the bulbous R-2 taxies away for takeoff. The foot-thick rudder shows up well here.

T. C. Weaver Collection

Contact, switch off . . . pulling the R-2's prop through had to be a back-breaking job.

T. C. Weaver Collection

Unusual overhead view of the R-2 shows the huge fuselage area compared to small wing area of the design.

Chris McGrath

him. He snap-rolled two times before returning to straight and level under control. Well, so much for tight pylon turns. He would fly the race straight and level, turning the pylons flat and wide depending on his greater power and speed to bring him first across the finish line. Had he tried the maneuver at normal racing altitude, fifty to one hundred feet, he would have wound up a careening ball of flaming wreckage. There would have been no room to recover. Now that he knew how to fly her, at least how not to get killed during one of her aerial rampages, he set about solving the next problem: qualifying for the upcoming Thompson Trophy Race. This was done by means of the Shell Speed Dashes, a daily event over a measured course. Since it was set up as an official F.A.I. course, it was possible to set a new world speed record as well as qualifying.

On Thursday, September 1, Jimmy poured the coal to the R-1 and hurtled through the traps at a speed of 293.19 miles per hour. That was great! It was a new record, except it was unofficial. Someone had neglected to fit a barograph in the plane to record the altitude. Worse yet, the cowl had pulled forward into the propeller, scuffing the paint job, splitting the metal in spots, snapping fastenings and stretching brackets. Further, there was a vibration problem with the Smith controllable-pitch propeller. He had caught the attention of the press, however; one story summed up the Doolittle R-1 team as "a stubby, sturdy pilot in a stubby, sturdy ship." With repairs

made to the cowling, Jimmy made a second attempt that same day for the speed record, this time with a barograph aboard. On this flight, with eyes watery from hay fever, he was unable to set a record, but he did horrify thousands of spectators who feared he would crash into a stand of trees at the north end of the field. After it was over, Jimmy scoffed, "I was nowhere near them." At this point, Doolittle and Grannie decided to call it quits on any further attempts at the record. They had qualified for the Thompson and both knew there was only so much time that an engine could run at a flat-out race setting without beginning to lose power. However, their efforts to save the engine almost became an academic episode.

On September third, Lee Gehlbach was taxiing the number 7 R-2 machine out of the hangar to set it up for photographs in the company of the R-1 parked near the edge of the field. He could not see over the bulbous fuselage and cowl and soon was headed straight for the R-1. Mechanics yelled and spectators screamed; arms were waved and crewmen tried to hold the R-2 back. Finally, though unable to hear the warnings, Gehlbach chopped the throttle as he sensed something had to be wrong, the ship was handling so sluggishly. It was then that he learned that if he had gone only another eight feet, both aircraft would have been damaged to the point the Granville racing effort would have been all over.

After that close call, Jimmy figured he had better get on with setting a world speed record before something else happened.

Lee Gehlbach, the 1932 R-2 Bendix pilot, poses beside his racing machine. Many consider him to be one of the finest racing pilots ever to have entered the sport.
C. Mandrake

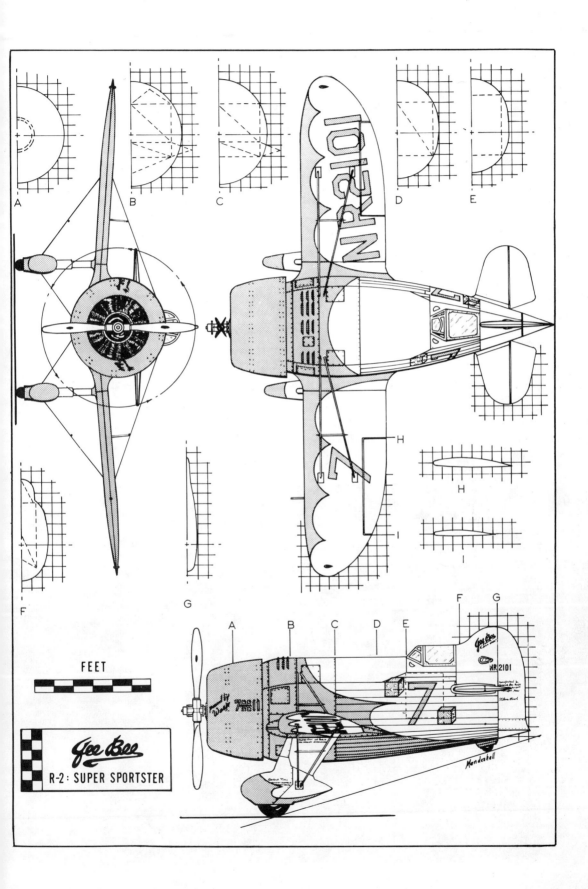

A B C D E

F G H I

FEET

Gee Bee

R-2: SUPER SPORTSTER

A B C D E F G

He climbed off into a gray, cloudy, turbulent sky and fire-walled her as the R–1 approached the Shell speed traps. The first of the required four runs was 293.047 miles per hour, then back the other way at 287.154 miles per hour. The third pass was a sensational 309.040 miles per hour and the last pass, against the wind, 281.966 miles per hour. The record was set—296.287 miles per hour was his official average.

During an interview after landing, he stated, "I left five miles more in her for Russ Boardman [who had been slated to fly the R–1 at Cleveland]. He can shoot the record up to more than 300."

Jimmy was doing great. Gehlbach, on the other hand, was having his problems—not of his own doing however. On take-off, shortly after nearly colliding with the R–1, a private aircraft landed directly across Gehlbach's takeoff path. It forced him

The R-2 gross weight when ready to roll in the Bendix was 3,883 pounds—2,000 of which was gasoline.

Pratt and Whitney

Jimmy Haizlip's Wedell-Williams '92' racer won the 1932 Bendix Trophy Race. Color scheme was black and white.

United States Air Force

to lift the R–2 off more quickly than he wanted. Fortunately, he had enough flying speed and missed the intruder by a foot or so. On the same flight, while attempting to run through the Shell Speed Dash course for his Thompson qualifying run, still another private plane appeared in front of him and he had to zoom up and off the course to miss him. Some days . . . He did qualify, however, at 247.339 miles per hour in the Dashes.

Event 7 of the Cleveland Nationals was a 1,000-cubic-inch free-for-all. Gehlbach, in the R–2 (which, with the smaller Pratt and Whitney Wasp Jr., was eligible), entered the race. He missed the first pylon and had to recircle it (shades of Roscoe Turner). This cut his average speed to 183.731 miles per hour and gave him only a third place. Jimmy Haizlip's Wedell-Williams '92' won at 203.405 miles per hour, and Jimmy Wedell in '44' took the second spot at 202.741 miles per hour. Gehlbach's winnings were $262. However, when you consider in those days that a new DeSoto 6 convertible was advertised for $675, it wasn't all that bad.

Except for the upcoming Thompson race, other racing events were now nil at the Nationals so far as the Granville organization was concerned. Maude Moriarty's (née Tait) Model Y engine was cantankerous and refused to run, so her bid for the Aerol Trophy was scrubbed. Frank Lynch offered his *Cicada* and they thought about giving her the R–2 for the race. It was finally decided that her lack of experience in either ship precluded her entry.

Monday, September 7, the final day of the Nationals, was also Thompson Trophy day. An hour before race time, it almost ended in disaster for the R–1. During a trial run-up, a carburetor backfire started a gasoline fire in the cowling. Fortunately, the mechanics and Doolittle promptly doused it, without any damage to the machine. The starting lineup was as follows:

PILOT	AIRCRAFT	RACE NUMBER	AIRCRAFT COLOR	POWERPLANT
Jimmy Doolittle	Gee Bee R–1	11	red&white	800hp P&W Wasp Sr.
Lee Gehlbach	Gee Bee R–2	7	red&white	450hp P&W Wasp Jr.
Bob Hall	Hall *Bulldog*	6	black&white	550hp P&W Wasp Jr.
Jimmy Wedell	Wedell-Williams	44	black&red	550hp P&W Wasp Jr.
Roscoe Turner	Wedell-Williams	57	red&cream	550hp P&W Wasp Jr.
Bill Ong	Howard *Ike*	3	white&gold	260hp Menasco
Ray Moore	Keith Rider	1	silver&black	260hp Menasco
Jimmy Haizlip	Wedell-Williams	92	black&white	550hp P&W Wasp Jr.
Lee Bowman	Israel *Redhead*	97	red&white	260hp Menasco

Victory is sweet as the floral-ringed R-1 is hauled past the Cleveland stands. The ship had just won the 1932 Thompson Trophy Race at 256.686 miles per hour and was flown by Doolittle.

C. Mandrake

When the starter dropped the red and white checkered flag, the most thrilling Thompson of all time got under way. The two Gee Bees and the Hall *Bulldog* lept forward from the pack and were quickly off the ground, gaining altitude by virtue of their controllable-pitch propellers. On the other end of the scale, the Israel *Redhead* was sitting in its original position

on the ground gathering the others' dust—this was due to a last-minute engine problem. The rest of the ships were now in the air with Doolittle beginning to move rapidly forward with the R–1's superior power and speed. He passed Hall early in lap one and continued to build his lead. The racers whipped past the stands to begin lap two. Doolittle, still moving away and trailing black smoke, continued to lead the pack. The smoke was due to too rich of a mixture caused by improper carburetor jets used in an attempt to cool the engine. Moore's Keith Rider and Wedell's '44' were gaining on Hall, now in second place. Haizlip's '92' and Gehlbach's R–2 were fifth and sixth. Turner and Ong brought up the rear. By the end of lap two, the big red and white R–1 lapped Ong's Howard *Ike*. Jimmy Wedell's and Haizlip's Wedell-Williams both passed Hall, then Moore's Keith Rider blew its engine and dropped out. By lap six, Doolittle was close to lapping Gehlbach's R–1 and Turner's Wedell-Williams. Turner, by the tenth lap, had managed to pass Haizlip. Never once as Doolittle flew the wide, flat course he chose did there exist the slightest doubt of the race's eventual winner— the R–1. The ten-lap, one-hundred-mile race finished as follows:

PILOT	AIRCRAFT	AVERAGE SPEED MPH	PRIZE MONEY
Doolittle	Gee Bee R–1	252.7	$4,500
Wedell	Wedell-Williams '44'	242.5	2,500
Turner	Wedell-Williams '57'	233.0	1,500
Haizlip	Wedell-Williams '92'	231.3	1,000
Gehlbach	Gee Bee R–2	222.1	500
Hall	Hall *Bulldog*	215.6	–
Ong	Howard *Ike*	191.1	–

The 252.7 mile-per-hour closed-course race speed was not to be bettered until 1936 by the French government-sponsored Caudron racer.

Doolittle landed and taxied up to the winner's circle. As he opened the R–1's door to the cheers of 60,000 race fans, he was bothered. He wondered what he was doing there. The press photographers had followed his wife and sons everywhere during the races trying to get a shot of the horrified family's reaction when the R–1 went in, as most of them expected to happen. That was it! The next day, Jimmy flew the R–1 back to Springfield and put it in the hangar at Bowles Agawam. He later told friends, "I landed it, taxied it up to the line and gratefully got out." At the time, however, he reportedly told newsmen, "It is the sweetest ship I ever flew, perfect in every respect." Springfield that evening became the scene of an elated populace celebrating the news of the R–1's victory. They had reason to celebrate, for now they were not only even more famous but, in the case of the S.A.R.A. shareholders, again financially well rewarded.

As for Doolittle, he hung up his racing togs. He once wrote, "I have yet to hear of anyone engaged in this work dying of old age." In an interview in recent years, however, he did say

Jimmy Wedell in '44' took second place in the 1932 Thompson at 242.5 miles per hour—a full ten miles per hour slower than the R-1 winner.

that today's military pilots who are used to hot, unstable, high-performance fighters would probably be able to handle the R–1 safely—but as for himself, he figured he had used up all his luck.

Jimmy got out at the right time. His victory marked the high point in the Gee Bee's chronology. However, in Springfield, plans were already underway for stretching the R–1 and R–2 designs for higher speeds and greater fame.

1932 Wedell-Williams flown by Roscoe Turner took third place in the Thompson at 233.0 miles per hour.

Gee Bee

"Y" SENIOR SPORTSTER

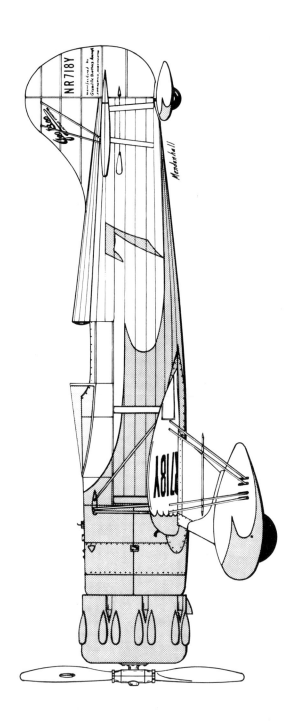

NR 718Y

manufactured by
Granville Brothers Aircraft
Springfield, Massachusetts

Mendenhall

1933 VERSION: FLOWN BY FLORENCE KLINGENSMITH: CHICAGO AIR RACES ......

5

Crashes and Crises

SNOW COVERED THE FIELD where Doolittle had lifted the R–1 off and icicles hung from the eaves of the ex-dance hall turned airplane factory. It was the home of the recently reorganized Granville Brothers Airplane Company. Long Massachusetts winters give plenty of time for planning and thinking. This was even more appropriate when you had the last two Thompsons in your pocket plus the world speed record. Grannie realized, of course, that the Gee Bee trademark now meant speed, speed and more speed to the world. This was fine from a superficial glamour standpoint, but it wasn't really the solid objective the company had started out with.

First there was the biplane, eight copies built. Then came the little Sportster, nine copies built. These were the stuff of which lasting aircraft companies were built, not one-of-a-kind specialty aircraft like the Z and R–1/R–2 planes. However, the racing end of the business had to be continued. The R–1 and R–2 parked in the shop were no doubt capable of far more performance if another year's development was expended on them. More horsepower would come first with the necessary modifications that the aircraft would need to accept it. They were on top of the heap—but hell, that rat race could go on forever with someone always ready to outperform you and send you sliding to the bottom.

Air transport, with fantastic growth potential, was where the future was. Therefore, the main direction of Granville Airplane Company from this time on would be as people movers, depression be damned.

There were the three-place R–5 Super Sportster International Courier, the C–4 Fourster, C–6 Sixter and C–8 Eightster. The number after the C indicated the proposed craft's passenger capacity.

The Eightster, for example, was projected with a forty-five-foot wing span, 390 square feet of wing area, and a new innovation for the Granvilles—fully cantilevered wing construction. The fuselage was thirty-four feet long. It was an enlarged version of the basic R–1 design with an anticipated top speed of 225 miles per hour. With a range of 870 miles there was more than enough room to carry eight people, including the pilot, from Boston to New York with a proposed new air service. Its cabin, because of the design criteria that the fuselage be larger in diameter than the 700 horsepower Wright Cyclone or Pratt and Whitney Wasp in order to build a giant teardrop, was twelve feet long, five feet high and five and a half feet wide. The four forward seats were full-swiveling and the craft featured forced-draft air ducts for each individual passenger—just like a 707. Also like a modern jet, there were individual reading lights, overhead storage, and window shades over the sealed windows for the faint of heart to close during a thunderstorm encounter. A single wheel of the throw-over type, à la Staggerwing Beech, was used to allow an unlicensed passenger to ride in the co-pilot's seat in accordance with Department of Commerce rules. Being a commercial transport, blind flying and cross country navigation instruments were also to be installed. With a wing

The clean, portly lines of the 1933 R-1 were a functional improvement over the 1932 model.

Granville Brothers Aircraft

loading of seventeen pounds per square foot, it was expected to land at only about fifty miles per hour using full flaps. A four-hundred-pound capacity baggage compartment under the cabin floor completed the transport. Since the cruise speed was only 190 miles per hour, it was possible to design the cowl for easy removal for engine maintenance—a good feature for a commercial transport. A Hamilton Standard controllable-pitch propeller was to be fitted and, lastly, a Granville must, fourteen coats of Titanine dope to hold the whole thing together.

Contemporaries of the slick speedster-turned-transport were such 'warts and all' workhorses as the Curtiss Condor, Ford Trimotor and the wooden-wing wonder, the Fokker F-3, in which Notre Dame's Knute Rockne met his death. However, this planning and preparation took time, so to keep the Granville name on the front pages, the racers for the moment would have to carry the load.

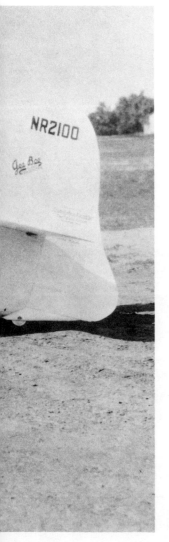

NR2100

Gee Bee

The National Air Races of 1933 were scheduled to leave Cleveland. They would now be held in Los Angeles early in the summer from July 1 through July 4. Further races were slated for later in Chicago during September and also at Indianapolis. These were to be the same caliber as the Los Angeles races. There was a lot of money and glory to be had that season. The two hot-shot Gee Bees (R-1 and R-2) were the great hope for making a bundle in these events. First, however, they had to be made over. The R-1 was updated with a bigger Pratt and Whitney Hornet engine. This meant a new, larger cowl to be hammered out by Hill Aircraft Streamliners. The Wasp out of the R-1 was put in the R-2 and a new, longer set of wings with landing flaps was built for the R-2. A carburetor air-scoop also blossomed under the cowl. With the increased torque of these new powerplants, the rudders had to be increased in area. This was gracefully done by adding the area to the lower portion of the rudder, still preserving the pleasing lines of the aircraft. A new tail wheel installation was made at the same time.

Russell Boardman was now recovered from his accident of the previous year and was once again pilot-elect for the R-1. As he was the chief shareholder in S.A.R.A., he asked for, and got, larger tanks installed in the R-1 so that the ship would be a viable contender in the Bendix as well as the Thompson Races. After being sidelined the previous year, by golly, he would take both the Bendix and the Thompson this year. Also, Doolittle said he had left an extra five miles per hour in her, even before modification—so he would have to give the world speed record a try during the Shell Speed Dashes. On March 25, Boardman flight-tested the R-2 and declared her shipshape. He then continued to fly both craft, the R-1 and R-2, regularly right up to race week in July.

In 1932, Russell Thaw, the Guggenheim family pilot and playboy, had given the Hall *Bulldog* the back of his hand. He was probably right, for soon after the Thompson, the ship was scrapped, once the instruments and engine had been removed. However, upon seeing the R-1 and R-2 perform at Cleveland, he showed a decided interest in the Granville products. He contacted the Granvilles to fly the R–2 during the 1933 season and was accepted at once. It was going to be a long Bendix race that year—New York's Floyd Bennett Field to the shores of the Pacific at Los Angeles—a lot longer than the previous Burbank to Cleveland races. A transcontinental speed record could be made with this one while still staying within the limits of the race course.

Finally, on July 4, the Bendix was underway with five hot racers vying to reach the West Coast first to collect the $10,000 first prize money awaiting. Frank Hawks was the official starter. The lineup was Thaw and Boardman flying numbers 7 and 11 respectively. Roscoe Turner was entered in his Wedell-Williams, which was now painted a solid gold color. Lee Gehlbach was flying the black and white Wedell-Williams '92' and lastly, Jimmy Wedell in his famous '44,' now red and black. Amelia Earhart was in the race flying a Lockheed Vega.

Takeoff order had been Turner, Gehlbach, Thaw, Wedell, Boardman and Earhart. Boardman didn't seem to have much lateral control and finished his takeoff run in the grass about fifty feet to the left of the runway. This was blamed on shock strut trouble. The five special race planes as opposed to the more staid Vega were flagged at a checkpoint in South Bend, Indiana, with Turner in the lead. Earhart was not expected to be seen until the longer-range Vega landed in Wichita.

At 6:05 A.M. Turner touched down at Indianapolis briefly

A beefed-up Gee Bee R-1 for the 1933 Thompson. Ship now had a Pratt and Whitney Hornet and a large rudder addition to counteract the increased torque and give better directional stability.

Arnold

for a ten-minute refueling, then was off again into the early morning western sky. Things weren't going so smoothly in Gehlbach's '92.' The engine gave up near New Bethel, Indiana, due to a fuel line vapor lock. There was nothing for Lee to do but pick out a likely field and make a dead stick landing. He collided with a fence, and a bent prop and bashed-in wing ended the Bendix race for Gehlbach.

Next in Indianapolis was young Russell Thaw in the R-2. He had taken off a half hour ahead of Boardman and was

Russell Boardman was the pilot of the 1933 Gee Bee R-1. He had the craft fitted with long-range tanks so he could fly it in the Bendix as well as the Thompson.

Granville Brothers Aircraft

Famous designer and race pilot Jimmy Wedell stands in front of his famous '44.' This duo was always ready to give the Gee Bee products a real tussle on the race course.

W. F. Yeager

supposed to go nonstop to Kansas City, one of two planned stops, but his fuel consumption had been higher than anticipated. The new wider and longer wing didn't help the ship's stability much either. Thaw was having trouble keeping the craft on an even keel as he made the approach. When he touched down, a wing dropped enough that it caught the ground momentarily and the ship swung into a wild ground loop. The wing tip was damaged but could be quickly repaired. Accordingly, the R–2 was hastily pushed into a hangar and work was begun.

Like the R-1, the 1933 R-2 now had more power with the fitting of a Wasp Sr. engine along with added rudder area.

Granville Brothers Aircraft

By this time, Boardman appeared in the eastern sky in the R–1, its big Hornet engine reverberating across the field as he came in hot. He had averaged 275 miles per hour on the flight from New York. He could have done better but wanted to save his engine for later. He was, of course, surprised to see the number 7 ship on the ground. Refueling began at once, and

Boardman and Thaw quietly conversed about the race and the fact that Turner was long-gone on the next leg west to Wichita. Finally, the R-1 was ready and Boardman taxied away, leaving Thaw pacing nervously in front of the hangar where the R-2 wing tip was being repaired. Thaw now paused to watch as Boardman ran up the Hornet to takeoff rpms and the ship began to roll. At 120 miles per hour and thirty-five feet, the R-1's nose pulled up into a rolling stall and plummeted back to the runway for a two-hundred-yard grinding slide before coming to rest.

Thaw, spectators and refueling crew drove quickly to the wreckage in the southwest portion of the field. Boardman, unconscious from head injuries, hung inverted from his seatbelt. The R-1's tail was lifted and Boardman was gingerly removed and rushed to the hospital. The R-1 was flipped rightside-up and towed to a hangar on its wheels. The top of the fuselage, cockpit, fin and both wing tips were heavily damaged. The field's weather station later said there had been a wind shift just as Boardman lifted off, causing the unstable, heavily laden ship to perform the disastrous maneuver resulting in the crash. To this day it is difficult to understand what kept the wreckage from catching fire. Another more likely version of the cause of the crash was that Boardman was too eager to get on with the race and had simply pulled the R-1 off too quickly and the torque got him. To confirm this, he had only used about forty percent of the runway and there were no obstructions ahead that required the early pulloff.

As a canvas was thrown over the plane, a shaken Russell Thaw said "the hell with it" and dropped out of the race. Boardman, in the hospital, had a fractured skull, punctured lung and broken shoulder. There was little they could do and, two days later, he died, never having regained consciousness.

Turner's luck continued to hold and he set the gold Wedell-Williams down in California after one last refueling stop at Albuquerque. Turner had set a new cross-country record. He had flashed over the grandstands just as the opening ceremonies were commencing for the National Air Races. Hot on his heels came Jimmy Wedell—so hot the times were rechecked to make sure the winner was indeed Turner. With '92,' the R-1 and R-2 out, that left only Amelia Earhart in her Lockheed Vega but she finally dropped out at Wichita, too far behind to be a contender.

Grannie had been waiting in Los Angeles for his two high-speed bombs to appear. Instead, he received the bad news that the R-1 was broken and Boardman lay dying in a hospital in Indianapolis and Thaw had even threatened not to fly the R-2 back to Springfield. The only plane left in the Granville stable at Los Angeles was the Model Y. Marty Bowman, a Burbank aviatrix, flew it to second place in the Aerol Trophy Race, winning just about enough money to pay for the gas used. Mae Haizlip won that race in the Wedell-Williams '92.'

Number 7 was flown by
Russell Thaw in the 1933
Bendix. On the New York to
Los Angeles flight, he got
only as far as Indianapolis.

Patterson

Fully modified for the 1933
Nationals with 425 horse-
power Pratt and Whitney
Wasp Jr., as well as elon-
gated, streamlined wind-
shield and landing-gear
legs smoothly faired over.

Gordon Williams

The Gee Bee Model Y just
before its modification for
the 1933 National Air
Races.

T. C. Weaver Collection

Grannie then entered the Y, which was now powered by a big Wasp Jr., in the Thompson Trophy Race. The competition for this one precluded him winning, but it was still worth a try for one of the lesser places. He was up against Roscoe Turner's Bendix-winning Wedell-Williams, Jimmy Wedell in the same type of plane, and Gehlbach who had patched up '92' for the race and flown it out of the Indiana cornfield dents and all. George Hague in a Keith Rider and Roy Minor in Howard's *Ike* rounded out the field.

The Thompson began with the usual racehorse start with Turner blasting past the scattering pylon and into the lead the first lap. Hot after him was Wedell, with Gehlbach, Minor, Hague and Granville strung out behind. Turner pulled one of his later-to-be-famous cut pylon acts on lap one but couldn't recircle it due to the rest of the pack rounding it. He made his own rule: he recircled it on lap two, then barreled around the course, recovering the lead over Wedell. Upon landing, after the race, he was awarded the winner's trophy. He then had to give it back. The judges ruled he had to recircle the pylon during lap one for it to have counted. Hence, Wedell was declared the winner. Turner was disqualified, and the others finished in the order that they had been strung out in the race. This meant Grannie got $375 prize money. All told, the prize money for the S.A.R.A. group was only about $1,000, and there certainly would be no more financial backing coming from Russell Boardman.

In September, over Labor Day, the Chicago National Air Races were held. It was at this race that Jimmy Wedell took over the world speed record at an average speed of 304.98 miles per hour, his best run hitting 316 miles per hour. His plane was powered by the Wasp that had powered the previous year's Gee Bee R–2. It was also at this race that the final blow for 1933 was again struck by fate at the now-tarnished Granville image. The second Model Y Senior Sportster had been purchased by Art Knapp from Lycoming where it was used as an engine

The final version of the Model Y being run up at the Chicago National Air Races.
Gordon Williams

Prior to Florence Klingen-smith's flight, the Y is pushed to the line.
T. C. Weaver Collection

test bed. Bob Hall assisted Knapp in putting a Wright Whirlwind engine in the craft, covering the front cockpit and placing an ultra-long, streamlined windshield in front of the rear cockpit. With the streamlined rocker-arm covers on the new cowl and the now-paneled-over openings of the landing gear legs, the Y emerged a sleek racing machine to say the least. Pretty, twenty-five-year-old Florence Klingensmith was to fly the Y in the Frank Phillips Trophy Race. This event was a bar-none free-for-all, not a lady's race, but she felt up to it. She announced over the

Zantford Granville and the R-1/R-2 Long Tail racer.
T. C. Weaver Collection

Hornet powered, the I.F. ("Intestinal Fortitude") was built from the fuselage of the 1933 R-1 and the wings of the 1932 R-2.
T. C. Weaver Collection

public address system before the race that she felt it would be a real challenge to take on the seasoned men pilots and she would give it her very best.

It must be remembered the Granvilles had nothing to do with this aircraft or pilot. The plane had been changed so much since it had left the Granville shop in 1931 that it bore little resemblance to the original, and it was now so overpowered the Granvilles wanted no part of it. After flying seventy-five miles of the one-hundred-mile race over a triangular course, and averaging over 200 miles per hour, Florence approached the home pylon. Instead of turning around it as expected, she kept going straight ahead and the crowds could see the fabric beginning to peel from the Y's right wing. After flying shakily for nearly two miles, the Gee Bee plunged upside down into a garden and shattered into pieces. Florence was found dead not far away entangled in her half-opened parachute.

Incidentally, the second Model Y built, Maude Tait's NR

Another bay of about two feet was added to the R-1 fuselage to accommodate the new larger conventional tail and tail skid.

Pratt and Whitney

11049, flat spun into the Atlantic, flying out of what is now New York's La Guardia Field. This accident resulted from a broken propeller blade that caused the engine to break loose from its mount due to vibration. Maude was not flying it. The R-2 number 7 that Russell Thaw had quit at Indianapolis in the middle of the Bendix race had been flown back to Springfield by Jimmy Haizlip who was now conducting flight tests on it. There was always the chance everything could be recouped at some later races. Haizlip met up with the same general touchiness that Doolittle had encountered the year before. During the flight, a slight amount of rudder movement gave such violent reaction that he slid across the polished red leather seat and slammed against the door. From then on, it was with a much tighter seatbelt and a much lighter touch on the stick and rudder that he flew the R-2.

This particular day, he wanted to show the Granvilles a fine, short field landing. He brought the R-2 in low over the trees at Bowles Agawam doing about 125 miles per hour indicated air speed. Haizlip put the ship into a side slip to kill off the excess momentum and altitude—a perfectly normal maneuver in a tail dragger. The next normal move was to straighten the plane out and let her stall gently onto its gear in a perfect three-point landing—except the cantankerous R-2 wasn't having any of that. In this case, at about a foot and a half off the ground, the left wing flicked into the ground as it started a snap roll. Haizlip had blanketed one side of the tail during his slipping maneuver. At zero altitude, a snap roll is bad business. This one resulted in a wing-tip-over-tail cartwheel down the field, ending in a completely demolished heap of junk from which a shaken Haizlip emerged. He had received only a minor head cut. "The blamed thing kept trying to bite itself in its tail," he reportedly exclaimed. Haizlip later said, "Pilots in those days felt that if another guy could fly the plane they could too so there wasn't much information on flying characteristics passed between them."

Well, there was still another cat that could be skinned for the remaining season and next year's Thompson Trophy Race— they still had some parts left. They had put a wider and longer wing on the 1933 version of the R-2 that Haizlip had reduced to scrap; therefore, they still had the set of wings of the same design that had been used on the 1932 R-1 and R-2. Someone in the group said, "Hell, let's combine the stuff we've got left into one plane—we'll be ready to race again."

The old R-2 wings were hauled out and attached in place of the two with broken tips from Boardman's aircraft. Since the crash had wiped out the 1933 R-1's fin and rudder, they extended the fuselage about two feet and constructed a new fin and rudder to fit the stretched airframe. This time, that portion was conservatively straight-forward. The rudder even had a trim tab. The tail wheel was disassembled and replaced by a long tail skid to improve directional stability on the ground. Streamlined rocker arm covers dotted the close-fitting cowling

surrounding the new Pratt and Whitney Hornet. For nostalgia, they hauled out the old good luck sign that had been painted on the Model Y (NR11049)—the crazy Filaloola bird whistling its incessant "gee bee, gee bee"—and painted it on the new ship's sides. With the catastrophes of 1933 still heavy on their minds, the words "Intestinal Fortitude" were emblazoned on the Hornet's cowling instead of the chancy dice of the earlier ships.

For a mulligan stew of leftover parts, the new ship, number 7, looked pretty much like a winner. They had made her number 7 to avoid having to repaint the wings which bore the license number NR–2101. The earlier Super Sportster troubles were thought to be conquered insofar as any inherent instability problems were concerned and she would be known as the R–1/R–2 Long Tail Racer. Yes, she would indeed give the now-rampaging Wedell-Williams machines a run for their money.

Roy Minor was to conduct tests on it in preparation for further racing. Accidents will happen, even to the best, and Minor was no exception. He had been brought east to handle the ship in the upcoming meet. Fine pilot that he was, even without experience in high-powered racers, he made his first flight with flying colors. A thunderstorm then hit the field, soaking things up pretty badly. On his second landing, after the storm, the brakes were ineffective on the wet grass and away he went, upending the ship in a drainage ditch. The cowl and propeller were damaged and the wing tips were bashed in, but Roy was unhurt—except for his pride. The Gee Bee was too banged up to be repaired for further racing that year. Thus, in the late fall of 1933, all that was left of the Granville Airplane Company was the beat-up "Intestinal Fortitude" and the totally shattered R–2 that had been hauled ignominiously off Bowles Agawam Field heaped on a stone boat for its trip to the dump.

Construction had begun on the Fourster and Eightster commercial models. They once were the major hope of the company as it had entered into 1933. Now, however, there was no more money to continue those programs so they were dropped. The Granville Brothers Airplane Company was sold at a sheriff's sale.

The I.F. retained the race number 7 to avoid the need of repainting the 1932 R-2 wings.

Pratt and Whitney

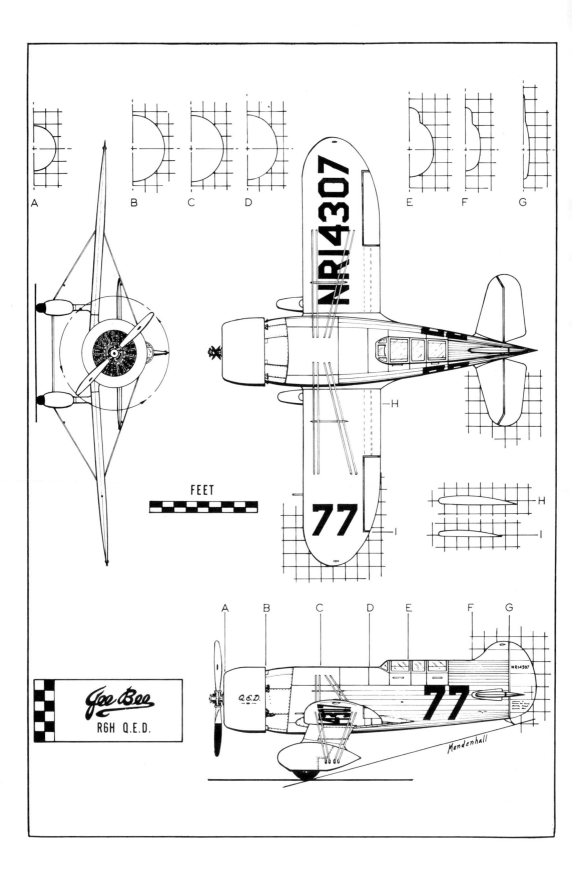

FEET

A B C D E F G

H

I

H

I

A B C D E F G

NR14307

77

Joe Bee

R6H Q.E.D.

Q.E.D.

NR14307

77

Mendenhall

6

Q.E.D.—Another Chance

WITH FINANCES, the 1933 racing season and their racing aircraft all shambles, less hardy men would have given up and gone to work for the WPA (Work Projects Administration) and leaned on their shovels. Instead, Grannie, Howell Miller and Donald DeLackner opened a consulting engineering firm at 101 Park Avenue in New York. Capitalization was $3,000, with $1,000 put up by each of them. It wasn't much but it would get them started.

The firm's first project was wild and flamboyant: an Indianapolis 500 racer! Grannie had gone to the 1933 Memorial Day classic and came away disturbed and completely disenchanted with the current state of race car designs—why, they didn't even streamline the car's underside. They just left the oil pan, transmission, differential, springs, and axles hanging out in the breeze, inducing drag all over the place. The blunt front ends and open driver's compartments didn't do much for his sense of aesthetics either. The three men's imaginations caught fire and they set about designing the dynaflow (years before Buick's P.R. people even thought of the name) design dubbed the 'Atlanta.' With a standard unhopped Ford V–8, the estimated speed of their sleek creation was 140 miles per hour. The car they created was teardrop in shape (what else?), three-wheeled with a massive fin and rudder. The two front wheels were the drivers and, of course, the whole bottom of the car was covered by a flat, smooth pan. An enclosed multi-paned cockpit smacked of the greenhouse of a DC–3. On models and plans, the whole creation carried the familiar red and white scalloped paint job. The final layout was completed by DeLackner on December 14, 1933, and included such specs as 122½-inch wheelbase, fifty-six-inch front tire tread and a racing weight of 2,500 pounds.

With great enthusiasm they were ready to start building the project—really a low-flying Super Sportster without wings! Then the bubble burst. Captain Eddie Rickenbacker wielded the pin. The president of the Indianapolis Speedway dropped by one afternoon at 101 Park Avenue. He looked at the project and said to Grannie, "I've got something to tell you. The

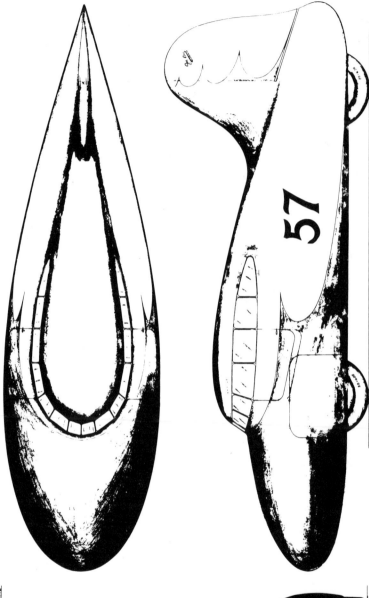

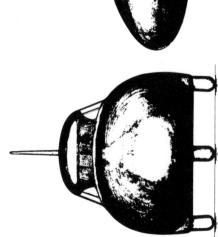

Gee Bee
"ATLANTA"

POWERED BY STOCK FORD V8 ENGINE
140 M.P.H.

WHEELBASE ---------------- 122½'
TREAD (FRONT WHEELS) ------ 56'
OVERALL LENGTH ----------- 227'
OVERALL WIDTH ------------- 64½'
HEIGHT AT RUDDER ---------- 84'
HEIGHT AT CABIN ----------- 64'
SEAT WIDTH --------------- 40'
TURNING RADIUS ---------- 19¾'
WEIGHT EMPTY ------------ 1750*
RACING WEIGHT ----------- 2500*

A-105		THREE VIEW "ATLANTA" MODEL F-V8-1
		GRANVILLE MILLER & DeLACKNER

definition of an automobile is a four-wheeled vehicle." The radical and sleek Atlanta bit the dust, fortunately before getting to the hardware stage.

With the car project killed off, they were still in the aircraft engineering business and looking for work. Their initial $3,000 was not going to last forever. Out of nowhere tragedy once more swooped down, this time taking the life of Zantford 'Grannie' Granville. He was slated to deliver a Warner-powered Sportster to a customer in San Antonio, Texas. Having had a rough year, both financially and emotionally, he had planned some fun interludes at the Florida races as well as the New Orleans Mardi Gras on the way to Texas. Foul, soupy gray weather pervaded the eastern seaboard and delayed his flight, time and again. Exasperated, he decided to just get the plane to San Antonio, to hell with the fun part. On February 12, he left Baltimore Airport on a southward leg to Spartanburg, South Carolina. After an uneventful flight, he let the little Sportster down on final approach to Spartanburg. Two construction workers were on the field in his flight path directly in front of him. He abruptly maneuvered to avoid them and in the process lost control. He spun in from seventy-five feet and was killed instantly as the aircraft disintegrated.

It is ironic that in that time period only two viable aircraft design groups existed in the field of all-out speedsters: the Granville organization and the Wedell-Williams people. They had vied closely for supremacy in 1931, 1932 and 1933 national speed events. On June 24, 1934, Jimmy Wedell was killed in the crash of a two-place biplane. His passenger was seriously injured. Here fate had taken its toll within a short period of time; the two greats in the speed merchant business died—but both prosaically in puddle jumpers, not the high-powered speed aircraft they pioneered.

While Grannie was still alive, however, a new hope had dawned for the company's future fortunes. The upcoming London to Melbourne Mac Robertson International Air Race with a first prize of 10,000 English pounds, about $50,000 in U.S. money, was something to really get excited about. Sir MacPherson Robertson had made a fortune for himself in the chocolate business in Australia. He decided to hype up a drive to open air routes to the 'down under' by means of a race. As it was, actually two Mac Robertson races were created. One portion was an all-out speed event. The other was a handicap contest for any type aircraft.

On January 5, 1934, Howell Miller completed a three-view general arrangement drawing of a new airplane: the Gee Bee International Super Sportster Model R-5. It had lines similar to the familiar R-1 and R-2; however, it was 'stretched' considerably larger with a span of thirty feet and a length of twenty-two feet six inches. It was to be powered by a Pratt and Whitney Hornet that developed 850 horsepower. It was expected to have a top speed of 295 miles per hour. Cruise would be at 250 miles per hour for 1,850 miles. It seemed to

Yes, there was a Gee Bee car design—for a short time. It came off Don De Lackner's drawing board in December 1933.

Granville Brothers Aircraft

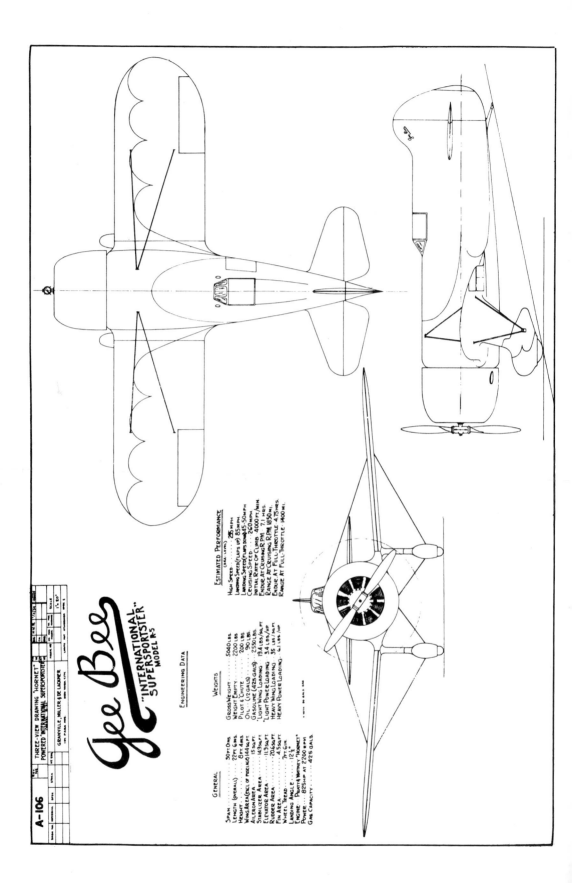

be a likely candidate for the Mac Robertson race.

Members of the aviation fraternity frequently dropped into the company's Park Avenue office when they were in New York. So it was that Jacqueline Cochran came by one afternoon. She was interested in an aircraft for the upcoming Mac Robertson race to Melbourne, Australia. She had planned to fly her Curtiss Conqueror-powered Northrop Gamma in the event, but the engine and supercharger were not performing well, so she needed a good backup plane. It was fortunate she did this, for the Gamma was cracked up prior to the race. Oh, well, it was only money!

Miller's International Sportster was shown to her and she liked the deluxe racer, except she thought perhaps a Curtiss Conqueror would be a better engine. Why she would want this is anybody's guess, as it was certainly opposed to the ideas for aircraft design according to the Granville concept of teardrop shapes. She worked with Miller as he redid the R–5 International Sportster into the R–6 which included a massive Curtiss Conqueror V–12 engine. The end result was, for all practical purposes, the 'Q.E.D.' as it was eventually built except for the engine. Q.E.D. is a Latin term usually first encountered in a high school plane geometry class. It stands for Quad Erat Demonstrandum, meaning "it is proven." As later events were to *prove*, they could not have picked a bigger misnomer.

To the Granville and Miller design team's relief, Curtiss found it was unable to deliver a Conqueror engine in time for the race. It was back to the radial Pratt and Whitney that Miller had wanted all along. Design predictions, based on calculations and experience, showed the ship would be faster powered with a Hornet anyway. With the design finally frozen and Cochran putting up the money, construction got underway. After a while Jackie did have one more request. She wanted a pressurized cockpit. Her reason was that she and her copilot could fly nonstop from London to Bucharest. This meant clearing the Transylvanian Alps with safety, and that meant flying at 18,000 feet. An expert from the Wright Field Division of Engineering was called in as a consultant, and after examining the drawings and fuselage, now being built, nixed the idea and suggested the Q.E.D. crew wear oxygen masks instead. Miss Cochran reluctantly agreed.

As it emerged from the shops, the big Lucky Strike green (Miss Cochran was a Lucky Strike girl in that cigarette's magazine advertising) machine looked very much like its predecessors— only a whole lot bigger. It had not been designed completely as a racer however. It met all Department of Commerce requirements for a commercial rating. Since there was still time to fly the ship in the Bendix as a sort of long-distance shakedown, orange racing numbers 77 (with a black pinstripe) were painted on along with the license number NR14307.

An inspection, starting with the wing, revealed the following information: Its span was thirty-four feet three inches with an area of 212 square feet; the two wing halves were rigged

Predecessor of the R6H Q.E.D., the Model R-5 Gee Bee came off Howell Miller's drawing board on January 5, 1934. Though never built, the design contributed heavily to the Q.E.D.

Granville Brothers Aircraft

to the fuselage with a two-degree angle of incidence and a dihedral angle of 4.5 degrees. Interior construction of the plywood covered wings, according to the company's general specifications for the R6H, went like this: "The wings are somewhat different from conventional design, but similar to racing practice design. The front spar is in reality two closely spaced, spruce beams with the landing and flying wires pulling between them, eliminating any eccentricity. The rear spar is a single beam with the wires pulling from the heat treated compression tube which also serves as an aileron hinge. Maple patch plates and steel bushing washers provide ample bearing for the wire pull fittings. Similar patches were provided to increase their bearing area. Ribs are of plywood web and spruce cap strip design, closely spaced and rigidly attached to both spars. The airfoil is a recent N.A.C.A. development, modified to give increased rear spar depth at the wire pull point, and a tapered tip. No drag wires are used, the plywood skin carrying the sheer load. Ailerons (which had an area of 21.2 square feet) are of similar construction to that of the wing, with an added torsion spar behind the hinge spar (and controlled by ballbearing mounted torque tubes). Flaps (as patented by Z. D. Granville) are built into the wing and extended from the aileron to the inboard end of each wing panel." The flaps were built in two pieces so that at full flaps the front one-third portion was down thirty degrees while the rear two-thirds were deployed sixty degrees. This type flap, as will be seen, gave tremendous lift

Painted Lucky Strike green, the color for the Q.E.D. was tied in with its owner, Jackie Cochran, who was a "Lucky Strike Girl" in the tobacco company's advertising.

Mitchel

and drag at the same time but could cause problems for the uninitiated. Two sets of stainless steel streamlined flying and landing wires kept the wing in rigged position. It is interesting that the flying wire type arrangement was used as Miller had already developed a full cantilever wing for the now defunct C–8 Eightster. Perhaps since this was a speed machine, it was felt there would be less drag with the thinner wire-braced air foil.

An engine had finally arrived—a Pratt and Whitney R–1690 Hornet that could belt out 675 horsepower. The propeller was a two-bladed Hamilton Standard controllable-pitch unit that had become standard for almost all of the powerful racers built. The Pratt and Whitney was cowled in a two-piece NACA cowling that was readily removable for servicing. With the previous experience of cowls pulling forward into the prop of the R–1, Miller wasn't about to have that happen again. He designed two heavy tubular rings, one located forward, the other aft of the cylinder bank. The cowl halves were attached to them. In addition, he added four radial rods from the crankcase nose section to the cowl's leading edge. Fresh-air intakes for cockpit ventilation, oil cooling radiator and oil tank, and, of course, carburetion, were fed through the pressure-type engine cooling baffles.

The fuselage, as was *de rigueur* in the Gee Bee engineering department, was enlarged to a sixty-one-inch diameter, well back from the trailing edge of the cowl. This was a continuation

With orange Bendix race number 77 on her flanks, the 675 horsepower Hornet is run up by Lee Gehlbach at Springfield prior to a test flight.

United States Air Force

of the perfect teardrop streamlining theory they held. The cavernous space between the engine and cockpit held 400 gallons of fuel in three tanks: the 275-gallon main tank, a one-hundred-gallon auxiliary tank right behind the firewall, and a twenty-five-gallon gravity-fed emergency auxiliary tank. The main tank was fitted with a dump valve so that it could be rapidly emptied and used as a flotation chamber should the ship be forced down over water. The twenty-eight-gallon oil tank and the oil-cooling radiators were also located in this portion of the aircraft.

Behind the tanks was the tandem two-place cockpit that was covered with shatter-proof pyralin panels. Sliding side windows were provided that could be opened and locked in any position. Adjustable seats and rudder pedals were made to allow some comfort on the intended long flights. Space was provided for two sets of removable controls, as well as dual engine and navigation instruments. Positive-level fuel gauges were installed. Fold-down side panels, fitted along the aircraft's left side at the seat positions, were for easy entry. The rotund fuselage was so roomy that, in addition to the items mentioned, there was still room for three separate baggage compartments.

Construction of the fuselage was generally in the same style as the R–1 and R–2. A welded chrome molybdenum tube frame was produced with stub fittings integral for wing attachments. The fin was also built integrally with the frame. To build up the teardrop shape, plywood formers were used with spruce

Jackie Cochran's big green machine sets in a hangar in Mildenhall, England, awaiting the start of the London to Melbourne Mac Robertson Race. Race number 46 is on her fin.

stringers, and the whole assembly was fabric covered. The areas around the cockpit and forward fuselage were aluminum covered. The fin was plywood covered, its area a miniscule 3.7 square feet. At the hinge line, it was nearly a foot thick. The rudder, like the R–1, was a built-up wood structure covered with plywood. Its area was 10.5 square feet. The stabilizer was full cantilever and mounted to the fuselage with the front spar being the hinge point and the rear spar connected to the trim link that moved it up and down. The elevators were of plywood covering, too, and were controlled by a push-pull rod, unlike the rudder, which was cable controlled. Respective areas of the stabilizer and elevator were 24.5 square feet and 15.6 square feet.

The landing gear tread of 7.5 feet looked a little narrow for good ground handling and tracking on that size aircraft. The streamlined pants enclosed the thirty-one-inch tires and wheels but did not move up and down as had been the case in the previous Gee Bee designs. The wheels, attached to long-travel oleo struts, used a modified Curtiss A–12 Shrike treadle gear. A streamlined section steel tube ran between the stationary portion of the two gears to absorb side landing loads. Cable-controlled mechanical wheel brakes were also provided. A long cantilever tail skid with a replaceable shoe completed the landing gear.

As the big ship sat glistening with its smooth, glossy paint job outside the Springfield dance-hall turned hangar, she could have been bought for $23,065.24.

With a new 825 horsepower Hornet up front, the Q.E.D. could get up and go at 295 miles per hour! It cruised at 260.
Miller

Lee Gehlbach, who had flown the R–2 in the 1932 Bendix, was chosen to do the testing of the R6H Q.E.D. He was also to fly it in the 1934 Bendix Trophy Race where they would see what she could do. Only nineteen hours after his initial test flight, Gehlbach pointed the Q.E.D.'s long nose toward the West Coast and, hopefully, a crack at fame and fortune, the same as in the good old days of 1932. She was a good ship and ready to race.

Arriving in California, Lee surveyed his competition. There was Roscoe Turner with his now-famous gold Wedell-Williams number '57' and Doug Davis, of 1929 Travel Air *Mystery Ship* fame, flying the late Jimmy Wedell's red and black '44.' John Worthen had the new retractable gear Wedell-Williams '45' that sported full cantilever wings. This ship had for a while been considered the prototype of the Army Air Corps' P–34 fighter. The dark blue Vance Flying Wing was there, still full of unresolved problems. It was flown by Lieutenant Murray Dilley. The new, sleek Keith Rider R–3 was an intended entry but flipped on its back during takeoff when the propeller caught the runway tarmac and killed pilot Jim Granger. Lee Miles, later to be named number one racing pilot after the 1934 racing season, would have flown the Wedell-Williams '92' but it had fuel tank problems.

With all these misfortunes, there still seemed to be the makings of a great race and perhaps a chance the Q.E.D. might emerge triumphant. This was not to be. In fact, the Bendix race of 1934 turned out to be one big fiasco. The only planes that even got in the air were Davis in '44,' Gehlbach in Q.E.D. and Worthen in '45.' Gehlbach found he had cowling troubles in spite of the massive measures Miller had taken to keep the cowl in place. He finally landed at Des Moines, Iowa, and had the troublesome thing removed. After that delay, plus the lower flying speed without the cowl, his arrival at Cleveland was too late for him to even be counted as a participant in the race. The cowling was flown in and reinstalled but the big green giant spent the rest of the races as a hangar curiosity. Jackie Cochran did not want her pride and joy flown in any of the closed-course events. There was too much of a chance of smashing her up and the Mac Robertson London to Melbourne race was coming up very soon. She did, however, allow it to be displayed and, in all truth, many fans were awed by the big, beautiful racing machine.

Davis in '44' and Worthen in '45' came in one and two in the Bendix, a real testimonial to their late builder, Jimmy Wedell. Davis, however, proceeded to get himself killed after a high-speed stall in '44' during the Thompson Trophy Race a few days later. The Nationals were over.

Gehlbach flew the Q.E.D. back to Springfield to be made ready for the Mac Robertson race. Jackie Cochran was philosophical about the Bendix debacle. The race had been used as a tryout rehearsal and had turned up the cowling problem.

Better to learn of it now than high over the Alps or the Malaysian jungle. After some rework, including some added fin area and installation of landing lights in the wheel pants, Lee Miles and Ed Granville flew the plane to New York where it landed near the docks. In fact, it was able to taxi to within fifty feet of the liner *Mauritania* that was to transport her to England. Fully assembled, it was lifted by crane to the liner's deck where it was securely lashed down. Ed Granville went along with the Q.E.D. to supervise the final work on it that would be required for several days after its arrival in England. The voyage turned out to be a rough one fraught with storms and heavy seas. At one point a hole was punched in a wing, but the damage was quickly repaired while still at sea. Once docked in England and the aircraft prepared, Jackie Cochran and her copilot, Wesley Smith, prepared to make the flight to Mildenhall, a London suburb from which the Mac Robertson race would originate.

Soon they were in the air for the short flight. As they lined up on final approach, it was getting dark and many eyes were on the big ship as it came over the fence, with landing lights blazing from the wheel pants. They dropped full flaps at about thirty feet, and the Q.E.D. literally dropped out of the air with a resounding thump. Smith, with typical English stiff upper lip, remarked to reporters, "You shouldn't think too much of it. It always lands that way." However, deep down, because of his and Jackie's inexperience with flaps, he knew that they

A span of 30 feet and length of 22 feet, plus the teardrop girth, made the Q.E.D. a big plane on the air race circuit.

Miller

should have applied them more gradually to get the feel of them. But publicly he referred to the flaps as "the clutching hand variety," and complained they spoiled the airflow over the ailerons. They did, if used incorrectly. More than once the big ship was dumped-in heavily for that reason. Many high-lift devices are great for delaying a stall, but if it finally happens —look out! However, the beefy Curtiss military landing gear took it all in stride and stood up under the punishment.

The initial landing in Great Britain did not help the green giant's image much, and there was already a barrage of insults being flung at it from the English press. More seriously, some questions came up about it receiving an air worthiness certificate because of the relatively small amount of test work that had been done on it. It had had only the briefest of test hops, then had been flown to the West Coast and back during the screwed-up Bendix business. After that, it was over to New York for the boat trip. For a commercial aircraft, that was a pretty light program.

The English notion of a race plane went something like the very sleek twin-engine de Havilland Comet—not the bulbous beer-barrel Q.E.D. The American entry was called such things as the "HeeBeeGeeBee" and more to the point, "ugly and dumpy." Obviously, the honest-to-God threat by the Q.E.D. to the English Comet entries (which eventually did win the race) was behind the bad-mouthing. Jackie Cochran and her copilot Smith were spared any cheap shots at themselves, however; in fact they were well liked for their conservative manner. This was in contrast to the flashy, uniformed showman of showmen, Roscoe Turner. Finally the Air Ministry relented and the Certificate of Airworthiness papers were issued. At the same time, race number 46 was assigned. This was neatly painted in black on a white oval on the Q.E.D.'s fin.

The United States was well represented with a multitude of aircraft from various manufacturers. These included the Douglas DC-2; a KLM ship; Boeing 247-D (flown by Roscoe Turner); Bellanca 28-70; the redoubtable Vance Flying Wing; Lockheed Orion, Vega, and Altair; Northrup Delta; Beech Staggerwing A-17E; Vultee V-1A; and Monocoupe 110 Special.

European manufacturers were equally well represented. The British fielded a de Havilland Dragon, Leopard Moth and Fox Moth, a Percival Gull, Short Scion, Miles Falcon and Hawk Major, Airspeed Envoy and Courier, Fairy 111F and a Harkness and Hillier monoplane. Their main thrust, though, was the super-sleek twin-engined de Havilland Comets, with three of the sleek and beautiful craft in all. The Comet would shortly be the prototype of the World War II great, the de Havilland Mosquito, one of the best combat aircraft ever built.

The French had a couple of entries, the Bleriot 111-6 and the Desautter Mark II. The Italians fielded a Bergamaschi PL-3 and the Dutch had a Pander mail plane. Thinking of this last group, it is beyond comprehension how anybody could put the Q.E.D. down from an appearance standpoint after being confronted with these aeronautical hags. Other aircraft had been entered but never arrived for the start. Of the ones present, attrition took its toll and not more than twenty finally took to the air at the beginning of the race.

The Q.E.D., with Jackie Cochran and Wesley Smith aboard, took off with a single flight and a horrendous landing by way of experience with the green giant since they had first met it thirty-six hours before. They were seventh in the starting order. After a long, long takeoff run, the heavily laden ship made a bobbling climb-out, attesting to the crew's inexperience and the plane's testiness when overloaded. Setting course for Bucharest, Hungary—a long flight that included leaping the Alps— they hurtled eastward over unfamiliar, even dangerous territory. Guts they had. When they arrived at Bucharest, those damned flaps would not work. One would come down but the other only partially. After three passes at the landing strip, they said the hell with it and set the Q.E.D. down. They were safe but the stabilizer was broken—a three-day repair job. This delayed the London to Melbourne race for Smith, Cochran and the Q.E.D. to the point that they were out of the contest. Jackie made her way by land back to London while Smith stayed with the plane. After repairs were made he demonstrated it to some Rumanian officials and obtained some vague promises that they might buy a few. This demonstration bit had been hatched many months before when Grannie had offered

1,000 horsepower, courtesy of Pratt and Whitney Hornet, a gold paint scheme and H. J. Heinz Company as sponsor all helped Roscoe Turner win the 1934 Thompson.

Carter

Cochran a nice percentage of any sales she might make of the
Q.E.D. to the European military during demonstrations while
the plane was in Europe.

Only four planes arrived in Melbourne to finish the high-
speed portion of the contest. The winner was the red de Havilland Comet *Grosvenor House*, the next was the KLM Douglas
DC-2, and the third was Roscoe Turner and Clyde Pangborn
in the Boeing 247-D. The handicap racers arrived, if they did
arrive, over the next week.

Smith's sales efforts in Rumania remained nil even though
he set a speed record on October 27 with that country's Prince
Cantacuzene aboard. Back in New York, the Q.E.D. capped
off its nothing career for the year by crash landing (those flaps
again) with Chilean Air Force officials aboard.

All years of Gee Bee history were incredible if not successful. First, the All American Derby in 1930, the *City of Springfield*
in 1931, the Doolittle/R-1 smasheroo in 1932, the wipeout in
1933 and now, in 1934, the death of Grannie, the "Intestinal
Fortitude" taxiing into a drainage ditch, the company's bankruptcy, and the Q.E.D.'s anemic record. When it rains, it pours!

At this point, with the Q.E.D., the last true Granville Brothers
aircraft, down on its luck, a few things should be said in retrospect about them. For one thing, the materials, engineering,
and construction were indeed first class—not even the slightest
hint of shoddiness was in their building. The problem with these
designs, if there really was one, was the fierce desire to push
constantly ahead into unknown frontiers. This type of activity
has always been a costly regime in both lives and money and
still is today. When one considers that only one each of the
futuristic and bold designs were built, the engineering had
to be top notch. There was never any going back to correct
mistakes after the prototype crashed and pointed the way to
corrections. The reason Granville Brothers Airplane Company
is not up there with McDonnell-Douglas, Boeing and Lockheed
is just sheer, concentrated bad luck for the most part.

The last of the Wedell-
Williams racers was the
Model 45 retract-gear job
with full cantilever wing.
The Army gave it the desig-
nation XP-34.

HAWKS' "TIME FLIES"

"Time Flies"

R
1313

Mendenhall

R1313

Pratt & Whitney
TWIN WASP
Hamilton Standard
CONSTANT SPEED
PROPELLER

HOWELL MILLER'S STUDY IN STREAMLING - 1936

7

Time Flies and Fizzles

THE Q.E.D. AND THE R-1/R-2 "Intestinal Fortitude" were entered in the National Air Races of 1935, and the R-1/R-2 was the first to continue with the dogged bad luck that had plagued the Gee Bees almost from the start.

Roy Minor, it will be recalled, taxied the "I.F." accidentally into a drainage ditch, upending her. While not severely damaged, it was impossible to repair it for the 1934 Nationals. Cecil Allen purchased the dented bomb with the backing, of all things, of a religious magazine and named the plane, *Spirit of Right*, and had the name painted on the sides. At that point, he was in good shape, but like almost all those backyard engineer/race pilot types, he decided to 'improve' the machine. First, he enlarged the cockpit canopy for better visibility while the aircraft was being completely overhauled. The scalloped paint job on the wing was replaced by a single red stripe down its leading edge—still no great shakes from an aerodynamic standpoint. Then came the clinker: Allen wanted more fuel aboard for the Bendix. The only space left was aft of the center of gravity. Howell Miller's calculations showed the center of gravity should not exceed twenty-five percent of the chord, and the additional tankage was going to push it back much further than that limit—thirty-five percent or even thirty-seven percent! Miller wrote him several letters offering his engineering information and help. Allen chose, for some reason, to ignore this extended helping hand. Disastrous results were soon to follow.

The fog hung low as the 1935 Bendix race got under way from Los Angeles to Cleveland. Royal Leonard was flying the Q.E.D., and Roscoe Turner was back in his famous gold Wedell-Williams with a rebuilt fuselage. More prosaic was Amelia Earhart in her Lockheed Vega, Roy Hunt in an Orion by the same company and Russell Thaw in a Northrop Gamma. Earl Ortman finally had the slick retract-gear Rider R-3 in a major race and last, but certainly not least, was the master of air racer design, Benny Howard, featuring his *Mr. Mulligan*, a beautiful white, four-place design, with Gordon Israel riding shotgun as copilot.

With the sky dark and scuddy, Cecil Allen gave the big Gee Bee hybrid a kick in the tail and she thundered off down the runway, the Hornet roaring a husky song of power. Spectators saw that his takeoff seemed to be very erratic and the plane appeared hard to control. Within a couple of miles the wildly wallowing Gee Bee fell out of the air, disintegrating in a beet field and killing Allen instantly. Once more a Gee Bee racer design was blamed for the pilot's death. Bayles, Boardman, Klingensmith, and now Allen. Unfortunately, the press ate this type of thing up without stopping to find out how the plane was deliberately modified against the advice of the Granville engineering department.

The Q.E.D. for a change got off to an excellent start. Royal Leonard had left in great style and was burning up the course. Then the new Hornet engine began falling apart at the seams and Leonard finally had to land at Wichita. Repairs could not be made so he had to drop out of the race.

Cecil Allen runs up his R-1/ R-2 *Spirit of Right* at Burbank a few days before the 1935 Bendix Trophy Race.

T. C. Weaver Collection

It turned out to be the Benny Howard Air Races instead of the Nationals that year. The slippery *Mr. Mulligan* took both the Bendix and the Thompson, with the little Howard *Ike* taking the Greve, making it a clean sweep of the three major national contests. Turner, Thaw, Hunt and Earhart finished the Bendix in that order.

About all that was now left around Springfield of the earlier Gee Bee days was the expertise for designing and building fine, fast racers. Frank Hawks decided to put that expertise to use. Hawks (with that name he *had* to be an airman) had made a name for himself the previous ten years or so with his wit, warm smile, good looks, daring, and string of distance speed records. He was all the things that heroes of the innocent thirties were made of, and just to make sure of his manly image, he also smoked a calabash pipe that must have held a quarter pound of his favorite mixture.

His famous Travel Air Texaco Special was obsolete and threadbare. He switched to a big Northrop Gamma but even that was getting old and lumbering compared to the status of the current crop of speedsters. Having seen the Q.E.D., he couldn't help but appreciate its range and fine finish, but his requirements included one additional ingredient: super speed.

He got together with Howell Miller who was delighted to oblige when told of the requirements. It would be the first high-speed aircraft he could do exclusively himself. With Grannie gone, the Granville, Miller and DeLackner group had run out of steam and had been disbanded. Miller, now operating with young Mark Granville, used other members of the old Springfield team only on a part-time basis as required. It was now Miller and Hawks with a new company formed for the occasion, the New England Aircraft Company. Miller was president, Hawks, vice president, and the Gruen Watch Company had agreed to foot the bills. Incidentally, the final bill on this new project came to $70,000—just a third of the cost of the only other plane that could hold a candle to it. That was the Hughes H-1 designed by Dick Palmer for Howard Hughes. The Hughes designer had unlimited funds from the multimillionaire flyer to work with. In spite of this, Miller's end result could not in the slightest be considered less of a craft than the H-1. In fact, its rate of climb was greater and it had a slightly longer range. If it had any problem at all, it was that Miller's brainchild still used conventional methods of construction versus the pioneering all-metal monocoque construction of the H-1, but even the Hughes aircraft had plywood wings.

Hawks worked right alongside the others as they built the sleek new aircraft. The drawings by Miller had shown a remarkable degree of streamlining but, as it took shape in real life, it was hard not to stand in awe of its slickly sculptured beauty. The team worked well together, everybody pitching in to do everything right down to sweeping out the shop. Unfortunately, due to the bad economic climate, the three remaining Granville brothers, other than Mark, still had to seek employment

elsewhere. The actual site of the new aircraft's construction was the same dance pavilion that had been used by the Granville Brothers Airplane Company for the R–1 and R–2. Grannie's spirit must have smiled benignly from the rafters as he looked down on the beehive of activity below. Hawks, for his part, also acted as night watchman, sleeping beside the plane in the hangar.

In many respects, while basic engineering was worked out by Miller for the design initially, Hawks himself made design contributions usually in the interest of getting more speed out of her. Miller, however, always kept a hard line whenever safety or structural integrity became a compromise. Miller had begun design work on June 12, 1936. Four months and six days later, they rolled their speed machine out of the shop—a truly super attractive creation. There was never a more sleek design built until the jet age produced the Lockheed P–80 Shooting Star. All glossy white with a perfectly smooth surface on wings, fuselage and tail, her lines were the epitome of the artistic side of aircraft design. Against the white background, the bright blue registration numbers stood out boldly on the wings and rudder as well as the flowing script name, *Time Flies*, on the fuselage flanks. A large blue-on-gold Gruen insignia shield appeared with the name.

Miller's idea of speed obviously encompassed a powerful engine, in this case a military-rated Pratt and Whitney Twin Wasp R–1830 that developed 1,150 horsepower. Use of that

In 1935 Cecil Allen purchased the R-1/R-2 and changed the canopy and windscreen, as can be seen in this photo. 'I.F.' is now off the cowl.
Strasser

The Hornet roaring with power, the chocks set, the R-1/R-2 is run up by Cecil Allen at Burbank prior to the 1935 Bendix cross-country race.
C. Mandrake

Cecil Allen strikes a relaxed pose aboard the ill-fated R-1/R-2 *Spirit of Right* before the 1935 Bendix.

engine required special governmental permission. A big three-bladed, ten-foot six-inch diameter constant-speed propeller, and an inertia starter, completed the powerplant end of this machine.

In keeping with the old Gee Bee design philosophy (a teardrop is the most perfectly streamlined shape) the largest fuselage diameter was at about the wing's leading edge. A very unique feature of the craft was the absence of a windshield and cockpit protruding into the airstream. Instead, with Hawks's approval, the ship was fitted with a flush-to-the-top combination windshield and canopy that was raised along with the seat by means of a manually operated three-dollar chain store hydraulic jack. During landings and takeoffs, the pilot's head was above the fuselage protected by the raised canopy that formed a windshield. In the air and at altitude, visibility didn't matter that much so the pilot simply jacked himself and the seat down,

Benny Howard's famous _Mr. Mulligan_ won both the 1935 Bendix and the Thompson Trophy Race.
W. F. Yeager

making the windshield a flush canopy with zero drag on the super sleek profile. Hawks once flew it at over 300 miles per hour with the seat and windshield up as a test of its strength. A teardrop-shaped side window added some additional visibility to either side.

Built the same as all the Gee Bee racers before it, it had a welded chrome molybdenum steel fuselage frame with plywood formers and spruce stringers. The fuselage was covered with Haskelite mahogany plywood. Only the cowling and a forward fuselage area near the exhaust stacks were of aluminum sheeting. Cockpit entry was through the same type starboard side door as was used on the R–1 and R–2. Also like the R–1 and R–2, the fin frame was part of the fuselage and had plywood ribs and covering.

Several advanced items, aside from the normal engine and flight and navigation instruments, were in the cockpit. For that time period, the plane had such modern devices as an exhaust gas analyzer to check the correctness of the air-fuel ratio, an aperiodic compass, a gyro-magnetic compass and a Sperry auto pilot. They obtained the auto pilot late in the plane's construction, necessitating a lot of rework to install it. Hawks later used the auto pilot often on long flights and found he could maintain altitude within, give or take, fifty feet. This left him free for navigation and singing, which he did to while away the time. Forced air ventilated the cockpit through flexible aluminum ducts connected to openings in the wings' leading edges.

Also in the wings was an experimental antenna for the then-new UHF radio. As a backup, a traditional two-way radio was also aboard, its antenna unreeling from the fuselage tail cone. Hawks's call letters were KHAOP. Three large tanks holding 250 gallons of gasoline plus a twenty-five-gallon oil tank were installed between the aluminum and asbestos firewall and cockpit. Oxygen bottles, for flights above 12,000 feet, were also installed. Overall, the length from propeller hub to plywood-covered rudder was twenty-three feet six inches. The rudder was fairly thick at the hinge line. Also in the fuselage rear was a retractable lift handle similar to the R–1 and R–2.

The thirty-foot four-inch wing was full cantilever featuring a NACA 23015 airfoil with 2½ degrees incidence at the root. This tapered to an almost symmetrical NACA 23009 section at the tip, set at zero degrees incidence. The wing had 160 square feet of bridge-like construction that featured three spruce spars boxed with plywood plus a multitude of quarter-inch plywood ribs that were routed out for lightness. The ribs were spaced on about eight-inch centers with maple corner blocks. This framework, when covered with plywood, was extremely strong. The aircraft was stressed for an amazing 12 G's because Miller had heard rumors coming out of Pratt and Whitney that they were working on a 2,000 horsepower Twin Wasp. He wanted to be ready for it strengthwise if and when it became available.

The ten-foot-span stabilizer was also of boxed construction and plywood covered. Trim tabs were on all flying surfaces and were vernier set. Grimes retractable landing lights were mounted in the lower surface of the wings along with the under-surface patented two-stage flaps, as were used on the Q.E.D. Navigation lamps were on the upper and lower wing tips as well as either side of the fin.

With the complex wing structure to gain strength, there was a problem figuring out what to do with the inward-retracting eleven-foot-tread landing gear. A Crosley (remember those funny little cars of the thirties?) engine starting motor was used for the muscle to pull the gear up. It drove right- and left-hand Acme screw-threaded rods, one to each side. The rods attached in the midsection of each landing gear. Since a screw thread is not reversible, the gear was locked in any position it stopped. The Oleo shock strut moved up and down with the treadle

The cleanest aircraft ever built during the propeller age, *Time Flies* splendidly awaits Hawks for a record-setting flight.

T. C. Weaver Collection

mounted wheels while the rest of the gear was stationary. Mark Granville was given the gear retraction problem and he soon had a solution. The wheels themselves were tucked into the fuselage since the wings were not thick enough to handle them. Wheel well covers smoothly buttoned the gear up. To finish off the landing gear, a small wheel for hard surface runways was fitted inside the streamlined tail skid used on turf airstrips.

Performance of this glossy white beauty was fantastic. It could climb out well over a mile a minute—7,000 feet per minute to be exact. Once trimmed out, she could hurtle along at 375 miles per hour or loaf at a cruise speed of 340 miles per hour. If he chose to use it, Frank Hawks had a record setter that would zap anything going in those days.

As this building activity was going on in Springfield, the Q.E.D. was being readied for the 1936 Thompson Trophy Race. Lee Miles, superstar of the 1934 races, was booked to fly it. There was a good chance the big green machine might win. Both Ben Howard and Roscoe Turner had washed out their machines during the Bendix. Howard's *Mr. Mulligan* and Turner's Wedell-Williams both lay on the southwest desert, scrambled heaps of cloth, wood and tubing, giving the Indians something to shake their heads at and wonder about the sanity of the white man. Two great thunderbirds had gone to the happy hunting grounds but the palefaces within had survived to fly another day. The biggest threat was Earl Ortman and the hot Pratt and Whitney Wasp Jr. powered Keith Rider R-3. Other contenders were the warmed-over Rider R-1 and R-2. Then, of course, there was stunt ace Michael Detroyat flying the mystery super-bomb financed by the French government—the dark blue Caudron C460. Under Detroyat's expert piloting it walked away with the Greve Trophy Race in which other small craft had been entered. Hoping the Caudron would drop dead as it raced around the pylons ahead of them were Art Chester in the *Jeep*, Harold Neumann in the Folkerts SK-2 *Toots* and Marian McKeen in the Brown B-2 *Miss Los Angeles*. They were all out-classed by the big iron, but who can ever tell how an air race will come out.

To make a long story short, Detroyat's Caudron won all the marbles—the Greve and the Thompson. Miles, flying the Q.E.D. for all he was worth, had averaged well over 200 miles per hour for eleven of the fifteen laps. Then came the engine giving up the ghost and the pullup off the course and out of the race. So much for another year of frustrating Q.E.D. racing. She was a classic grand old gal that could move out pretty good but, certainly for closed course racing, was now out of her class when faced with the newer, slender retract jobs being fielded by their prize-hungry designers.

It might be mentioned that there was one big angry howl let out by the American backyard pilot/builders, with their threadbare pocketbooks, concerning Detroyat and the Caudron funded by the French government coffers. No other foreign country ever came back. Even Howard Hughes backed away

from entering the fabulous H–1 in competition with these guys.

Meanwhile, on October 15, Hawks reviewed the *Time Flies* and asked Miller if the finished ship was ready. Miller assured him it was done and to have no qualms about flying it. Both Miller and Hawks had their fortunes and reputations riding on the beautiful machine and, perhaps, a military contract if it turned out as good as they expected. The same day, Hawks cautiously began taxi tests, runups, the whole gamut of tryouts prior to an initial flight. At 3:07 P.M. he buckled up his parachute,

The prop looks big, and it was—a massive ten-foot six-inch constant-speed Hamilton Standard product. The seat jacked up and down with the windscreen.
Cooke

A low front three-quarter-view camera angle is always good for an airplane's appearance. For *Time Flies*, it is exquisite.
T. C. Weaver Collection

took a deep breath, and opened the throttle. Rolling rapidly, she quickly lifted off and handled like the thoroughbred that she was. After a couple of circuits of the field so the builders could see their creation flying, he set a course for nearby Hartford and Rentschler Field where the runways were longer and United Aircraft had engine and propeller mechanics near at hand. Once on the ground, in front of the Gruen brass that had bankrolled the airplane, Mrs. Hawks christened *Time Flies* officially. The Springfield guys were a little miffed by this turn

Time Flies **sits squarely on her ten-foot six-inch tread retractable landing gear. Tail skid had a wheel inside for use on paved runways.**
T. C. Weaver Collection

With the windscreen down, this three-quarter rear view shows off the high degree of streamlining *Time Flies* **had. It had a 30-foot 4-inch span and an overall length of 23 feet 6 inches.**
T. C. Weaver Collection

Time Flies abuilding—sans engine—in the old Springfield dance hall.

With the skylight up, *Time Flies* still looks fast—and she was. Frank Hawks flew her at over 300 miles per hour like this.

Even without wheel covers and landing-gear fairing, *Time Flies* still looks like a sleek champion speedster.

T. C. Weaver Collection

Two teardrop windows, instead of the original one, were seen on *Time Flies* after Hawks's original landing accident. The purpose was to better judge landing attitude.

T. C. Weaver Collection

No hangar queen, the Hawks *Time Flies* sits in shiny white splendor with blue markings during a fix-up for a speed-record try.

C. Mandrake

A big R-1830 Pratt and Whitney Twin Wasp powered *Time Flies*. Special permission had to be obtained from the U.S. Army Air Corps to use it.

T. C. Weaver Collection

The French Caudron C-460 made a shambles of the 1936 Greve and Thompson races for the American contestants in 1936.
W. F. Yeager

Clayton Folkerts designed the SK-3 for Rudy Kling who promptly went off and won the 1937 Thompson Trophy Race with it.

The first year out for Roscoe Turner's LTR-14 was 1937. Even with no wheel pants, he came in third in that year's Thompson Trophy Race.

of events. They had wanted the christening at their field. Hawks, however, was in no way going to jeopardize his little jewel going in and out of that short hayfield.

By December 23, the ship had an hour and fifteen minutes of testing on it without incident. Leaving well enough alone, Hawks took the holidays off and did not return to the air until January 6, 1937. That was a bad day as he could only get the landing gear halfway down. The irreversible screws held, however, and combined with Hawks's 'walking on eggs' landing, *Time Flies* suffered only superficial damage to the wheel covers and the three prop tips. What caused the malfunction? Hawks's fur-lined gloves had fallen into the gear mechanism, jamming it. Hawks was really upset about the incident and wrote a letter to the Navy warning them about the possibility of similar accidents in the retract-geared Grumman biplane fighters.

While they were fixing her, they added another tear-drop window to the port side for better landing visibility. Hawks was growing older and was not quite so flamboyant as he was in his earlier years with Texaco. When it came to *Time Flies*, particularly after the accident, he was extremely cautious. Everything he had was tied up in the ship. It even took him a while to pay off Miller for his work. He made several trips to Anacostia Naval Air Station to show the speedster to the military. While its performance impressed them, they felt the design was obsolete. They were now playing with all-metal Seversky P–35's and Curtiss P–36's and this ship, though indeed beautiful, was

just too flimsy for the robust military life. Miller had been forced to build with the materials he used because of the lack of metal-working equipment in his shop. He hoped to redesign the ship as an all-metal aircraft if he got a government contract. Hawks, still cautious with his 'white hope,' waited until spring and good weather for a distance flight. In February he logged only two test flights, with another in March and seven in early April. All tests were limited by the weather and a lack of daring on the part of a pilot growing older. As the saying goes, "There are

With race number 61 applied, the overhauled Q.E.D. looks forward to the 1938 Bendix race.
C. Mandrake

Charles Babb acquired the Q.E.D. in late '37 and overhauled her for the 1938 Bendix. Color was white with green trim.
Strasser

old pilots and bold pilots but no old, bold pilots." Hawks wanted to grow old. Perhaps he should have farmed the ship out to a fearless young Turk who would pull out all the stops and set record after record, including the world speed record, with the ship. The aircraft was capable of it. It could have even won the Thompson or Bendix.

The best he could do, however, was gird his loins on April 13, 1937, and hop off from the East Hartford airport and set course for Miami 1,304 miles away. On course and on Sperry auto pilot,

The Q.E.D. caught with her flaps down! Here they appear to be a single unit rather than the double unit used earlier by Jackie Cochran.

T. C. Weaver Collection

The Babb-acquired Q.E.D. could do over 300 miles per hour with its new 875 horsepower Pratt and Whitney Hornet.

Strasser

the speedster slipped southward, quickly landing in a record four hours and fifty-five minutes, and in time for lunch. Refueled, he headed back north to Newark and for dinner in New York. Four hours and twenty minutes later he entered the pattern at Newark. He had raced north at 15,000 feet, averaging 240 miles per hour. His tanks were nearly empty and he was in a hurry to get down before dark, perhaps hungry for that New York dinner. He blew the whole ball game. The plane bounced so hard and high on initial contact with the runway it was 200 feet before he landed permanently. The third bounce had been accompanied by the resounding crack of wing spars giving way. As *Time Flies* came to a stop, the right wing hung limp like a crippled bird. The landing gear was also bent up. It was 6:56 P.M.

Someone always tries to place the blame elsewhere when there is an accident, and this episode was no different. "A faulty spar" was the cause said some self-appointed engineers who had witnessed the accident. Faulty spar indeed—it was stressed at 12 G's! An extremely poor landing was more like it. It is very doubtful Hawks enjoyed his New York dinner that night. In fact, he probably didn't eat at all, for this was the end of the rope. He was out of money. Gruen was totally disenchanted with the lack of favorable publicity and swept the whole project under the rug. That was *Time Flies'* last flight and Hawks had her trucked back to "Hawks Nest," his home in Redding, Connecticut. He stored her in a barn there—a proud, proud bird

Over four years old, Babb's Q.E.D. still looked fit and ready for racing.

T. C. Weaver Collection

in a turkey hutch. Total flight time was a meager twenty-seven hours and forty-six minutes.

The rest of 1937 saw nothing by way of activity for the Gee Bee line. The Q.E.D. had been purchased by aircraft broker Charles Babb and was getting a complete overhaul for the 1938 Bendix cross-country contest. She wasn't eligible to be in the Thompson because a new rule had been established preventing the same plane from flying in both races. Nineteen thirty-seven was the first year no Gee Bee plane appeared in the listings of National Air Races events.

George Armistead, a Babb employee, was to fly the new Q.E.D. in the 1938 Bendix. Here he runs up the big Hornet.

C. Mandrake

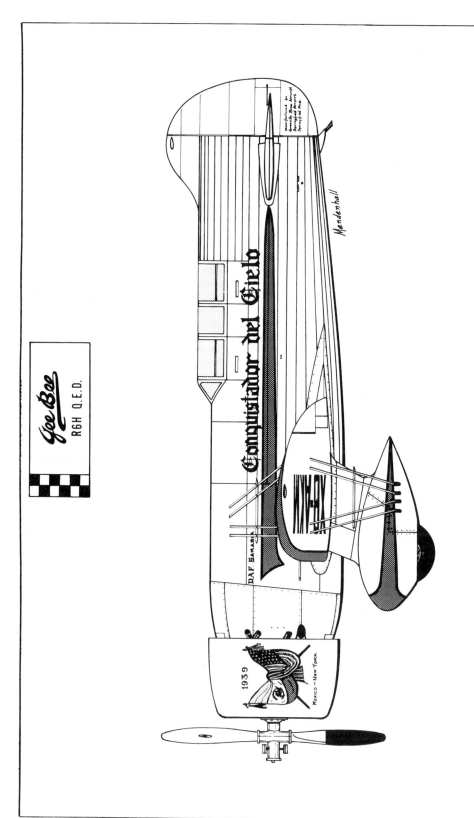

Gee Bee
R6H Q.E.D.

Conquistador del Cielo

XA-ANM

D.A.F. Sarabia

1939

Mexico — New York

Mendenhall

manufactured by
Granville Bros. Aircraft
Springfield Marrifc
Springfield Mas.

SARABIA'S R6H AS DISPLAYED TODAY AT CIUDAD LERDO, MEXICO

8

Double Trouble

TIME FLIES HAD GAINED some notoriety and was much too valuable to leave stashed in a backyard barn. A new firm, Military Aircraft Company, was formed. It went slow and money was scarce in the spring of 1938 when Hawks entered into a sales contract with Tri-American Aviation. That concern was headed by Edward Connerton and Leigh Wade. Wade was the Army pilot who had flown the Douglas World Cruiser *Boston* in the first round-the-world flight. Tri-American wanted an aircraft that was a prototype of a fast attack ship. They were looking for sales in South America or possibly war-beleagured China. *Time Flies* and its spare parts were returned to Springfield and Howell Miller joined the group.

Repairs to the broken wing and landing gear were quickly accomplished and a new, long AT-6 type greenhouse (with many small panes) was added far back on the fuselage. A dark blue and gold paint scheme (or black and yellow, depending on who is recalling the aircraft) was sprayed over the all-white machine. The darker color was used on the fuselage and fin, the lighter shade on the wings and stabilizer. It was renamed the Hawks Military Racer HM-1, with new license number NX–2491. A smaller fuel tank was installed along with dual controls. Room was made for a couple of fifty-caliber Browning machine guns in the wings. A gun mount in the rear seat was also designed for that occupant, with an interrupter gear to prevent blasting off the plane's plywood tail in a hail of lead.

Saddened and disillusioned by his *Time Flies* experience, Hawks had announced he was giving up speed flying. Not wealthy, he still had to work, so he took a part-time position as a demonstration pilot with the Gwinn Aircar Company. Gwinn was trying to develop an everyman's aircraft, a car that flew and was foolproof in the process. The fat little biplane demonstrator, which had a small four-bladed propeller and tricycle landing gear, took off on August 23. Hawks was piloting and a potential financial backer was his passenger. There was a wild attempt to fly between some trees and under a high tension line. Hawks and the backer were killed.

Leigh Wade made the initial test flight of the HM-1 the same day Hawks and his passenger met death in the Aircar. The ship was now fitted with a Pratt and Whitney Twin Wasp Jr. of 900 horsepower. The old 'landing gear not coming down' bit came up again. This time it was due to asbestos from the firewall getting jammed in the mechanism. After a great deal of work, Wade got it down and made a successful landing. After one more test flight, Wade flew the HM-1 to Cleveland for a chance at picking up some money at the National Air Races.

Meanwhile, the Q.E.D. was now repainted cream with a green stripe on its fuselage sides and wheel pants. It was undergoing an overhaul by aircraft broker Charles Babb, who had purchased it for the 1938 Bendix race. When completed, it was to be flown in the upcoming Bendix by George Armistead, one of Babb's pilots. Armistead flew the plane to Texas for a long-distance shake-down flight. The plane now had a 950 horsepower Pratt and Whitney Hornet under the cowl with

Time Flies **was turned into the Military Aircraft HM-1. It was to be a lightweight fighter/attack aircraft with super-hot performance.**

a 14–1 supercharger and it could easily hit 300 miles per hour. Near Amarillo, Texas, Armistead had to make a forced landing into a soil erosion project because of engine trouble. No damage was done and soon he was on his way to Los Angeles and the start of the 1938 Bendix.

The race was on and Armistead left the Burbank Union Air Terminal heavily loaded with 400 gallons of fuel, which was enough to make Wichita in one mighty hop while he sucked on oxygen at 14,000 feet. His competition, and there was a lot of it, were off and running too. Frank Fuller, Jr. (the 1937 winner), and Jackie Cochran sported P–35 civilianized Seversky pursuits; powerful, fast and all metal. Three Staggerwing Beeches joined in, flown by Max Constant and Harold Ross in retract models and Bob Perlick in an earlier fixed and spatted gear version. Paul Mantz flew a Lockheed Orion and Frank Cordova flew the large, fast and long-legged Bellanca Tri-Motor powered by a big Ranger and two Menascos. Rounding out the gaggle was Charles La Jatte in an all-metal Spartan Executive and Lee Gehlbach in the perennial Wedell-Williams '92.'

By the time the Q.E.D. had sped over Kingman, Arizona, Armistead knew he had not been overlooked in the Gee Bee legacy of fickle fingers. Oil temperature was going up and the pressure was going down. Rain and sleet were causing carburetor icing which, along with a radio failure due to a twiddling knob falling off, ended his dreams of making Cleveland and a few bucks. He packed the whole thing in at Winslow, Arizona, walking away from the ship in disgust. Three others met the same fate; Gehlbach, Perlick and Cordova were dropouts. Jackie Cochran won, followed by Fuller, Mantz, Constant, Ross and La Jatte—strung out behind her in that order. The Cleveland terminus of the race was alive with another great thrill-packed racing meet. The high point of events was the unlimited free-for-all Thompson Trophy Race. Leigh Wade waited to try his luck in catching the gold ring astride the HM–1 in that one.

Pratt and Whitney had installed racing jets in the carburetor to keep the engine running cooler and richer, and this required some testing. The tests were to be monitored by Miller to check out fuel consumption. There was no point in turning left and going like hell only to run out of fuel before the race was over. The final strategy involved Wade holding off in the early laps of the race to conserve fuel. Then when he felt there was enough to complete the race, firewall the HM–1 and hopefully win. The best laid plans . . . Due to insufficient time for testing, Wade found he had used up more than half his fuel during the first half of the race. Flying a high, wide race, à la 1932 Doolittle, he found he had to cut back on power in order to finish, not open it up as planned.

Earl Ortman zapped into first place in the Marcoux-Bromberg Special followed by Roscoe Turner in his Laird-Turner LTR. Art Chester was coming along behind them in his new *Goon*, and Steve Wittman was pushing the much modified

Chief Oshkosh for all it was worth. Joe Mackey flew the old Wedell-Williams '92'; Keith Rider's latest, the *8-Ball*, was flown by Joe Jacobson and last was Harry Crosby in the sleek, little CR-4 retract job of his own design. Ortman's oil system gave up and Roscoe took the lead. Crosby and Chester dropped out due to mechanical problems. When the whole thing shook out, Wade was fourth behind Turner, Ortman and Wittman. Following him were Mackey and Jacobson. It had to be difficult for Wade who was forced to hold back to conserve fuel. It was a good thing he did, too, for the engine quit as he touched down at the race's end. Who knows what the HM-1 could have done had it really been able to get the bit in its mouth and *GO!* Turner won $22,000 and Wade won $2,500. Wade said, "to hell with air racing" and returned to South America, but only after wringing the ship out. At Dayton's Wright Patterson Field, he flew the HM-1 against some first-line experimental planes that were being tested there. The P-36A Hawk, the Seversky P-35 and others tried their abilities against the HM-1, but the HM-1 out-performed them every time. If it had been all-metal, a contract would have been forthcoming. Wade returned the ship to Cleveland, and from there Earl Ortman took it back to Springfield.

Since the race hadn't come off as planned, Earl Ortman was hired to do some testing of the HM-1 to try and gather data that would make it an imposing proposition to a foreign power as a super-duper military airplane. As an eye opener, a

Low three-quarter-front photo shows black fuselage and fin, yellow-gold wings and stabilizer.

Burton Kemp

twenty-five-mile course was set up between Rentschler Field and the Haddam Dam on the Connecticut River. Ortman was scheduled to make four passes over the course, which he did. This was done at a flashy average of 369 miles per hour—some eighty miles per hour faster than the sleek Seversky P–35. Miller smiled quietly at his vindication. Okay, the speed was wrapped up so now on to the climbing ability, which quickly showed the HM–1 was able to get upstairs at 6,000 feet per minute compared to the Air Corps' first-line P–35 rate of 2,000 feet per minute. It was a real skyrocket!

The next set of data needed was to determine climb rates and power settings from 1,000 to 11,000 feet. Well-documented data always helps back up the sale; it's impressive. Ortman was to try ten or fifteen different climb rates to 11,000 feet, then dive back to 1,000 feet to save time, and the cost of gasoline. To prolong endurance, an eighty-seven-gallon gas tank had been fitted in the back seat.

Up and down he went, feeding gas from the main tanks for the fuel-gulping maximum climbs. Meanwhile, the eighty-seven gallon tank went unused in the rear seat and the center of gravity crept silently toward the rear of the ship. As his final dive hit 425 miles per hour, the stick ripped out of Ortman's hands and the aircraft became uncontrollable as its tail tried to hit its nose. The violent stresses were too great. The wing spars failed and a wing ripped off, falling away in the slipstream. Ortman joined the Caterpillar Club at once and bailed out.

The wide stance of the inward-retracting gear precluded any ground-looping tendencies. Tread was ten feet six inches.

T. C. Weaver Collection

The HM–1 plunged to earth, totally disintegrating, digging a hole, and ending its career all at the same time. There would be no repairing this one and no building a new one. Ortman, for what it was worth, said: "The HM–1 was the fastest and best plane I have ever flown." Funds were nil and the crash killed any interest South America, China or the Army Air Corps might have ever had.

Miller, who during this period designed a light twin pusher called the *Moonship* as well as a couple of low-wing sport planes, went to work for Pratt and Whitney. The war was coming and, as the years went by, he worked in the area of research engineering.

Late in 1938, Charlie Babb got sick of looking at his hangar queen, the Q.E.D. It had never won a race, and in fact it never even finished a race. He sold it to his friend, Captain D. A. Francisco Sarabia who was called the "Lindbergh of Mexico" and who was also *el presidente* of a Mexican airline.

Sarabia decided to brighten the ship up a bit to his taste. He had her repainted a gleaming high-gloss white with red speed lines painted on the sides of the fuselage and wheel pants. In large, bold Old English lettering, the words "Conquistador del Cielo" were printed in red on each fuselage side above the speed line. These words translated into "Sky Conqueror," a misnomer if ever there was one. The United States license was, of course, changed to one of Mexican registration—XB–AKM. Crossed American and Mexican flags were painted on either

Racing number 41 was added for Leigh Wade's attack on the 1938 Thompson Trophy Race. He came in fourth.

Strasser

side of the cowling along with the year "1939" above the flags and the words "Mexico-New York" below them.

On May 8, 1939, Sarabia announced a flight in the "Sky Conqueror" from Mexico to New York as a good will gesture during the opening of the 1939 pylon and perisphere World's Fair. He would make the trip nonstop from Mexico City to New York, 2,350 miles, setting a speed and nonstop distance record. Just before 8:00 A.M. on May 24, the big Gee Bee lumbered off the Mexico City runway fully loaded with fuel, oil and personal messages from Mexico's president, Lazaro Cordenas, to Franklin Roosevelt, Fiorello La Guardia, and the governor of New York and World's Fair president, Grover Whalen.

For the stamp collector, there is a little side story here. Sarabia was carrying 400 commemorative postal covers, each marked with a cachet applied by the Mexico City Post Office depicting the Statue of Liberty and a Mexican government building. The stamp, a standard design Mexican airmail stamp, was specially printed in red and blue rather than the usual red and green. It also was inscribed with "Sarabia Vuelo Mexico-Nueva York." Though never offered for sale by the Mexican Postal System, 2,100 copies were printed—1,000 going to Sarabia for any use he desired. He sold a couple of hundred before the flight for about twenty-five dollars each—a guy has to get gas money from somewhere! The rest of the stamps were disposed of in the following manner: 400 to the Universal Postal System in Berne, Switzerland; 300 to Mexico's Philatelist Society; and

HM-1 finally crashed during high-speed dive tests flown by Earl Ortman. The HM-1 had done over 400 miles per hour in dives.
Burton Kemp

400 through the national lottery. The 400 special covers Sarabia carried were back-stamped in New York, and after a stamp collector tempest in a teapot, they are now recognized and sell commercially for $225 each in the market.

Heading northeast towards New York, Sarabia pulled the big ship up to 16,000 feet. All through the flight, there was a fight against head winds, with a couple of howling thunderstorms thrown in for good measure.

As the time for his arrival approached, a gaggle of newspeople, Sarabia's family and general spectators gathered at Floyd Bennett Field. There was some apprehension in the air due to the Q.E.D.'s checkered record of never finishing anything it started. As darkness approached, rumors started flying about a forced landing at Atlanta and about a sighting over Virginia.

From downwind came the whine first, followed by the bellowing roar of a flat-out Pratt and Whitney. He circled once to give everyone a good look at the "Conquistador del Cielo" really doing her thing and then settled for a smooth but hot downwind landing. The landing was downwind because he was plain out of gas—about a gallon left in the tanks. It was 6:40 P.M. Figuring time zones, he had been in the air ten hours and forty-nine minutes. He taxied up to the waiting crowd, popped the hatch and looked down. He stood up and smiled, assured of the hero's adulation that seemed to drive these fellows. "It was one of the toughest flights I ever made," commented Sarabia

to the reporters. The police then escorted him and his family into New York where he and the 'Little Flower,' Fiorella La Guardia, mayor of New York, exchanged greetings and compliments.

He was very delighted with the Gee Bee and offered to set the Granvilles up in Mexico building airplanes. He felt that a wood and tubing fabric-covered aircraft was much more able to withstand the tropics than the all-metal variety. Sarabia's business manager was present when Mark Granville and Howell Miller declined the offer.

Upon landing after the long flight, and out of gas, Sarabia said it was the toughest flight he had ever made.

T. C. Weaver Collection

One day was taken to rest up, then on the 26th, he opened the Mexican Pavilion at the Fair where, in halting English, he said, "It is rather unusual for me to speak in public. I am a flyer, not a speaker. But, I want to tell you the purpose of my flight. It was to bring a message of good will from the people of Mexico to the people of the United States."

Captain D. A. Francisco Sarabia, with an exhaust-stained R6H behind him, poses for the press.

T. C. Weaver Collection

The ceremonies over, Sarabia then flew to Washington for further receptions. Roosevelt, a stamp collector of note, was given a block of four of the special stamps for his collection, along with a small signed scroll stating: "With sincerest admiration for you as a noted statesman who has rendered distinguished service in the present era, I have the honor of dedicating to you this souvenir of my good will flight from Mexico City to New York City."

1938 winner of Thompson, the LTR-14 Pesco Special.

The submarine *Squalus* foundered soon after Sarabia had landed in New York. With many dead and some survivors

brought up in a diving bell, the sea drama pushed Sarabia into the inner portions of the evening papers. Fame is fleeting.

While Sarabia had been conducting his good will mission, the "Sky Conqueror" was housed in an Army Air Corps hangar at Bolling Field outside Washington. It was now 5:30 A.M. on the morning of June 7, 1939, and Sarabia was ready to return to Mexico. A group of his family, including his wife and son, chatted happily with him as he climbed in and fired up the big ship. With 250 gallons of fuel aboard, he lined up with the runway and opened the throttle of the big Hornet. Clearing the runway, he gained altitude to about a hundred feet when the roar abruptly stopped—silence. With the heavy gas load, the plane fell like a rock into the Potomac, flipping on its back and sinking in fifteen feet of water. Louis Quintamila and Commander Manuel Zermene, both Mexican officials, ripped off their coats and plunged into the river in a rescue effort. After several dives, they reluctantly had to give up. A crash boat and motor launch meanwhile had been dispatched to the scene by the base officer of the day who had been alerted of the crash by telephone. The site was 400 yards off the river's eastern bank and a mile and a half south of the naval air station. As had been the case with the Mexican officials, members of the crash boat crew were also unable to extricate Sarabia's body from the cockpit. The craft's nose lay stuck in the mud, its tail sticking out of the water about three feet. Lines were strung to the aircraft to try and right it but the sucking river-bottom mud held

The 1939 winner of the Bendix Trophy Race was Frank Fuller in his SEV-52 (P-35) Seversky.

The Wedell-Williams '92' soldiered on through 1938 on the air race scene though now badly outclassed by its opponents.

1939 winner of the Thompson was Roscoe Turner and LTR-14 at 282.5 miles per hour.

Roscoe Turner, winner of 1938 Thompson Trophy Race at 283.4 miles per hour.

fast. At last, with more boats hooked up, they moved her (but still underwater) and towed her tail-first to a dock. A dock crane then lifted her enough to bring the cockpit above the river's surface. Sarabia's head had been jammed through the windshield, his body held tightly in place by crumpled cockpit structure. Portions of the cockpit and windshield had to be cut away before his body could be recovered and released to the undertaker. The plane was then hauled out, and three hours after takeoff was back at Bolling Field banged up but still in one piece. As for Sarabia, the official cause of death was listed as drowning!

Yankee sabotage! The rumor quickly flared in Mexico. The Mexican people took the death of Sarabia, only thirty-nine, to heart and lashed out angrily. Guards were placed around the American Embassy in Mexico City to quell an expected riot and demonstration. Roosevelt, of course, sent condolences to Sarabia's family and the Mexican government and offered the services of the Army Air Corps to fly Sarabia's body home. That was accepted.

On June 10, at 3:30 P.M., the giant Boeing B–15 took off and flew to Mexico City nonstop in a little over twelve hours. A crowd of 200,000 gathered around the plane bearing their hero. Many of them were angry over the sabotage rumor and shouted, "Long live Sarabia and death to saboteurs." Twenty-five persons were arrested for throwing rocks at the plane. Sarabia's funeral attracted 300,000 people.

Five weeks later, the Air Safety Board released its investigation results. A rag, left inside the cowling by an unknown person (thought probably to be a mechanic), had been sucked into the carburetor, thus shutting off the engine's fuel supply. The board ruled out sabotage as they felt the rag could not have been fixed to stop the engine at the crucial time it did. It was a combination of stupid carelessness and fate going into play once more.

A big political hassle still swirled through Mexico with much hatred and accusations centering over the possible gringo sabotage. Santiago Sarabia, the pilot's brother, returned to Washington after the funeral and had the plane dismantled and shipped back to Mexico. It was stored, still crated, in a corner of a hangar owned by Sarabia's airline, which went out of business about 1943. It was then moved to the family farm and stored in a shed till the mid-1960's. Alberto Sarabia, the flyer's cousin, put up the money and had the craft restored to museum condition and erected a special building for it at Cuidad Lerdo across from the village park. So there it sits today, on a polished floor in Mexico, the last of the Gee Bee's. A proud, pristine bird, a monument, if you will, to the line of seven racing aircraft built by Granville Brothers Airplane Company in far-away Springfield, Massachusetts.

They were hot, fast and unlucky airplanes, but there was none that ever sat around waiting for a pilot wanting to thrill to the challenge of mastering them.

Tex Johnston's black and yellow Cobra II took the 1946 Thompson at 373.9 miles per hour.

In 1947, the Thompson fell to Cook Cleland in his blue and white F2G-1 Corsair. Speed was a hot 396.1 miles per hour.

1948 found Anson Johnson tooling along at only 383.8 miles per hour in his stock P-51D Mustang, winning the Thompson.

9

Enough is Enough

IT'S BEEN FORTY YEARS now since the last Gee Bee pounded down a runway and raced off powerfully behind a big, bellowing Pratt and Whitney. It was the end of the line, not only for the Gee Bee aircraft, but for the Golden Age of air racing as well. The first flickers of World War II came the same day that Roscoe Turner was ramming his LTR Special around the pylons to win the last prewar Thompson Trophy Race.

That day, Hitler's Stukas were pounding on the Poles. Within months, the whole world was embroiled in the conflict. The Battle of Britain unfolded, turning London into a fiery hell of death and destruction. Next came the sorry debacle of Pearl Harbor adding to the successful Axis thrust into France, Belgium and the low countries. The German armies and the Luftwaffe made a deep and powerful sweep into Russia as the Japanese overran the South Pacific.

Most of the Granville people went to work in the aircraft industry contributing their vast skills in the building of high-performance aircraft. Howell Miller went to Pratt and Whitney where they were putting the big radials together by the tens of thousands. The rumor he had heard about a 2,000 horsepower engine was indeed true, and it wasn't long before that engine was imparting super performance to the Republic P–47 and the Navy's counterpart, the Corsair. Bob Hall went to Grumman as did Gordon Israel. Benny Howard went to Convair and Art Chester to North American. Roscoe Turner opened a flying school where he turned out Flying Cadets by the score.

One of the first bright spots for the racing community and the nation was Jimmy Doolittle's return to the front pages when he led a group of carrier-launched B–25's in their famous thirty-seconds-over-Tokyo raid. The Germans had eventually collapsed under the blows of the massive Allied bomber fleets. The raids sometimes included over a thousand planes. Japan yet remained, but within a little over a year the atom bomb was dropped on Hiroshima and the Japanese succumbed within a week. The war raged for six years, finally ending in August of 1945.

By Labor Day the following year, 1946, the National Air Races were once more scheduled for Cleveland. A veritable air force appeared in that Ohio city's skies. Racing from the West Coast, as in the old days, came the Bendix contingent with a P–51 flown by Joe DeBona taking the event well over a hundred miles per hour faster than any previous Bendix winner. However, it was also a hundred miles per hour slower than the new jets that were beginning to dot the skies, fluffy contrails trailing behind them.

The Thompson was hot and hairy with a flashy yellow and black P–39 Aircobra flown by Tex Johnston taking the flag at a blazing 373.91 miles per hour.

By the 1947 Cleveland Nationals, it was evident that interest, while still there, was down a measurable degree. People became a little tired of the same old warplanes scrambling around the pylons. It certainly wasn't the days of the big Gee Bee setting down in Cleveland, a breathtaking spectacle of unknown speed and stability. Perhaps that is what made the Golden Age. Anyone with enough desire, ingenuity, guts and a little money could

Cook Cleland, once more the winner of the Thompson in 1949 race, in his highly modified F26-1 swept around the course for a win at 397.1 miles per hour.

design, build, race and win those early events. On the other hand, thousands of man-hours and millions of dollars went into the development of a fighter and somehow it all seemed so impersonal.

Around-the-world pilot Bill Odum appeared at the 1949 Nationals in a highly modified P–51 to take on the Thompson contest. It did arouse interest because of its extreme modifications. Called the *Beguine* after Cole Porter's great show tune "Begin the Beguine," it was painted a lustrous metallic green with the notes and scale of the well-known song painted in gold down the fuselage side. Most different, however, was the removal of the massive air scoop from beneath the fuselage. In its place were large cylindrical oil coolers on each wing tip which to the layman looked very much like ram jets. Unfortunately, it looked much better than it performed. Bill was killed when the P–51 went into a high-speed stall and crashed into a Cleveland apartment house, killing several of its occupants. This tragic event was the end of air racing because of public demand and outrage. Since that time, Reno and Mojave have been host to a few of the big iron World War II machines still flying today. Each year takes its toll in racing accidents, and eventually there will be none left to race.

It is very understandable why there is so little interest in these events today. It would have been the same watching a gaggle of Wright Flyers and Curtiss Pushers tooling around the pylons in 1939. Interest under those circumstances would have been practically nil. So the end has now come to the motor sport of air racing—for all practical purposes. That most demanding and exciting contest fades into the past. However, it is only a normal progression of events. Nobody races chariots or clipper ships much anymore either.

Appendix

The Gee Bee Data Bank

THE FOLLOWING SECTION IS PROVIDED as a quick reference source for dimensional and performance figures of the Gee Bee airplanes, by model, as well as the derivative *Time Flies* and HM–1 aircraft.

The Gee Bee Model A Biplane

This model was the first built by Granville Brothers Aircraft. In all, eight units were completed during the years 1929 and 1930. Its specifications were as follows:

Wing span, upper wing—29 feet
Wing span, lower wing—26 feet 3 inches
Wing area—185 square feet
Overall length—20 feet 7 inches
Height—8 feet 6 inches
Empty weight—1,060 pounds
Gross weight—1,650 pounds
Powerplant—Kinner K–5, five-cylinder radial air-cooled engine developing 118 horsepower. The initial prototype was powered with a Velie M–5 and at other times, for test work, a Chevrolair D–4 and Cirrus Ensign were fitted.
Maximum speed—108 miles per hour
Cruising speed—92 miles per hour
Landing speed—39 miles per hour
Rate of climb—800 feet per minute initially
Service ceiling—11,000 feet

In addition to a conventional landing gear, this aircraft was also offered with skis and floats. Passenger configuration was two place, side by side.

The Gee Bee Model X Sportster

This aircraft was the first low-wing model to be produced by the Granville organization. Lowell Bayles flew it to second place in the 1930 Cirrus All American Flying Derby. Its specifications were:

Wing span—25 feet
Wing area—95 square feet
Overall length—16 feet 5 inches
Height—6 feet
Empty weight—750 pounds
Powerplant—American Cirrus Hi-Drive, four-cylinder air-cooled inline engine with a DePalma supercharger developing 110 horsepower.
Maximum speed—145 miles per hour
Cruising speed—125 miles per hour
Landing speed—50 miles per hour

The aircraft was painted black and white in the typical Gee Bee paint scheme. Its license number was NR49V. After the Cirrus Derby, the airplane was fitted with a Fairchild 6–390 engine. This plane was the prototype of eight more Sportsters that were eventually built.

The Gee Bee Model B Sportster

This aircraft was the second of the Sportster series built and was powered with a 95 horsepower Cirrus Hi-Drive unsupercharged engine. Dimensionally, it was the same as the X. Painted tan and brown with a red pinstripe, its license number was NR854Y. Built for pilot Harold Moon, it differed from the Model X in engine cowling configuration and landing gear construction. While the X used a rigid gear with large donut tires, the B was fitted with shock absorbers and a semi-streamlined landing gear fairing. This increased the empty weight to 870 pounds.

The Gee Bee Model C Sportster

The third aircraft in the Sportster series, the Model C was painted red and white with a black pinstripe and license 855Y. It was built for George Rand and was powered by a Menasco B–4 engine that delivered 95 horsepower. In 1931, this ship was returned to the Granville shop and rebuilt to a Model D configuration. Changes included a new fin, rudder and a full streamlined panted landing gear.

The Gee Bee Model D Sportster

The fifth aircraft produced in the Sportster series was the Menasco C–4 powered Model D. The engine was 125 horsepower and gave the D a top speed of 150 miles per hour with a cruising speed of 130. Overall length, due to the engine, increased to 17 feet 3 inches. Landing speed remained at 50 miles per hour. The aircraft was painted blue and cream with a black pinstripe and was licensed NC11043. First used by Zantford Granville as a demonstrator, it was later acquired by several pilot/owners: Bill Rausch, Clem Whittenback, Dannie Fowlie and Mae Haizlip. The aircraft was fully aerobatic and could climb to 5,000 feet in four minutes.

The Gee Bee Model E Sportster

By far the most popular of the Sportster series, the Model E featured a 110 horsepower Warner Scarab radial engine. Of the nine Sportsters built, numbers 4, 6, 7, 8 and 9 were this model. The following is a description of each of these models:

Number 4 Sportster was Army yellow and blue with license number 856Y. The overall length was 16 feet 9 inches, six inches less than the inline engine versions. It was owned by Al Nott and later Zantford Granville. The landing gear was the faired type found on the earlier Model B.

Number 6 Sportster was red and white with a black pinstripe and was licensed NC46V. It was owned by William Sloan, Lowell Bayles, Zantford Granville and Russell Boardman, in that order. It was the aircraft in which Boardman was injured the week before the 1932 Thompson Trophy Race. The craft had previously been flown by Granville in a Los Angeles to Cleveland handicap race and by Bayles in the 1931 Ford Air Tour.

Number 8 Sportster was painted red and white with a black pinstripe and carried license number NC11044. It was owned by Skip Tibert and carried a full streamlined undercarriage.

Number 9 Sportster was green and cream with a black pinstripe and licensed NC72V. It was owned by William Sloan, Johnny Crowell, Don Walters and Jack Wyman, in that order. The wing for this ship is currently in the EAA museum and is red and white indicating the ship was repainted at least once after leaving the Granville factory. Another engine, later fitted to NR49V, was the 135 horsepower Ranger.

The Gee Bee Model Y Senior Sportster

Two Model Y Senior Sportsters were built in 1931. They were 'stretched' two-place versions of the original Model X design. They were both painted red and white with a black pinstripe. License numbers were X11049 (later NR11049) and NR718Y. Their specifications were as follows:

Wing span—30 feet
Wing area—138 square feet
Length—21 feet
Empty weight—1,400 pounds
Powerplant—Lycoming air-cooled radial R–680 delivering 215 horsepower.
Maximum speed—160 miles per hour
Cruising speed—135 miles per hour
Landing speed—55 miles per hour

NOTE: At least three other engines were fitted to these aircraft. A summary of them and their performance increase is as follows:

Powerplant—240 horsepower Wright J-6
   Empty weight—1,425 pounds
   Maximum speed—165 miles per hour
   Cruising speed—140 miles per hour
   Landing speed—56 miles per hour

Powerplant—300 horsepower Pratt and Whitney Wasp Jr.
   Empty weight—1,500 pounds
   Maximum speed—185 miles per hour
   Cruising speed—155 miles per hour
   Landing speed—60 miles per hour
Powerplant—425 horsepower Pratt and Whitney Wasp Jr.
   Empty weight—2,000 pounds
   Maximum speed—201 miles per hour
   Cruising speed—165 miles per hour
   Landing speed—56 miles per hour

The aircraft were both lost in accidents. Florence Klingensmith was killed at the 1933 Chicago International Air Races in NR718Y and the other was destroyed when a propeller blade broke off and the engine was shaken loose from its mounts.

The Gee Bee Model Z

The Z, *City of Springfield*, was the first all-out racing plane produced by the Granville Aircraft Company. Only one was built, though an engine change to increase speed was done in an attempt for the world speed record in December 1931. Its specifications were as follows:

   Wing span—23 feet 6 inches
   Wing area—75 square feet
   Overall length—15 feet 1 inch
   Empty weight—1,400 pounds
   Gross weight—2,280 pounds

Powerplant—535 horsepower Pratt and Whitney Wasp Jr.
  985
Maximum speed—270 miles per hour
Cruising speed—230 miles per hour
Landing speed—80 miles per hour
Range—1,000 miles
Fuel capacity—103 gallons
Oil capacity—11 gallons
Wing chord at root—50.4 inches
Wing loading—30.2 pounds per square inch
Dihedral angle—4.5 degrees
Angle of incidence—3 degrees
Aileron area—9.5 square feet
Horsepower to weight loading—4.26 pounds per horse-
  power
Stabilizer area—8.4 square feet
Elevator area—6.9 square feet
Fin area—2.2 square feet
Rudder area—4.9 square feet

The Z was painted yellow and black with a brown pinstripe.
Its license number was NR77V and the race number was 4.
With the revision to a new 750 horsepower Pratt and Whitney
Wasp Sr. engine, the plane was ready for a world speed record
attempt during which one pass was made at 314 miles per hour.

The Gee Bee Ascender

This aircraft was a canard design using the engine and wing
of an Aeronca C–2. It was ultralight with a tricycle landing
gear and single-place cockpit positioned in front of a large fin
and rudder. The aircraft was built in a week and was only flown
a few times during December 1931 before being scrapped.

The Gee Bee Tiger

Built in January 1932 by Edward Granville, the Tiger was a small,
low-wing aircraft similar to the Sportster, although somewhat
different in outline configuration. It was rather nose-heavy,
but it did manage to fly a few times before being dismantled.

The Gee Bee R-1 (1932)

The R-1 is without a doubt the most famous of all the Gee Bee racers. It was flown to victory in the 1932 Thompson Trophy Race by James H. Doolittle. Doolittle, in addition, also set a world's speed record with it during that same race meet. The color scheme was red and white with a black pinstripe. The license number was NR2100 and its racing number was 11. Its specifications were as follows:

Wing span—25 feet
Wing area—100 square feet
Overall length—17 feet 9 inches
Empty weight—1,840 pounds
Gross weight—3,075 pounds with full tanks; 2,415 pounds for racing
Powerplant—800 horsepower Pratt and Whitney Wasp Sr. 1344
Maximum speed—300 miles per hour
Fuel capacity—160 gallons
Oil capacity—18 gallons
Wing chord at root—53 inches
Angle of incidence—2.5 degrees
Dihedral angle—4.5 degrees
Maximum fuselage diameter—61 inches
Wheel tread—76 inches
Airfoil section—modified M-6

The Gee Bee R-1 (1933)

The R-1 was revised for the 1933 National Air Races to be able to compete in the Bendix as well as the Thompson Trophy Race. Modifications included a larger fuel tank for longer range and the installation of a new, more powerful engine, the Pratt and Whitney Hornet R-1344 that developed 800 horsepower. Additional rudder area was added to counteract the torque of this larger and heavier engine. Russell Boardman was killed in this machine on takeoff from Indianapolis, Indiana, during the 1933 Bendix Trophy Race.

The Gee Bee R–2 (1932)

The Gee Bee R–2, the sister ship of the R–1, was to compete in the Bendix Trophy Race. Flown by Lee Gehlbach, it came in only fourth in that race due to a cracked oil line. It was painted red and white with a black pinstripe. The license number was NR2101 and the racing number was 7. Its specifications were as follows:

Wing span—25 feet
Wing area—100 square feet
Overall length—17 feet 9 inches
Empty weight—1,796 pounds
Gross weight—3,883 pounds with full tanks; 2,371 pounds with 50 gallons of fuel for closed-course racing
Powerplant—550 horsepower Pratt and Whitney Wasp Jr. 985
Maximum speed—250 miles per hour
Fuel capacity—302 gallons in two tanks; 103 gallons in the front tank and 199 gallons in the rear tank
Oil capacity—20 gallons
Wing chord at root—53 inches
Angle of incidence—2.5 degrees
Dihedral angle—4.5 degrees
Maximum fuselage diameter—61 inches
Wheel tread—76 inches
Airfoil section—modified M–6

The Gee Bee R–2 (1933)

The R–2 was modified much as its sister ship, the R–1, was. A larger engine was installed; in fact, the Pratt and Whitney Wasp Sr. that had been used in the R–1 in 1932. To improve directional stability, the rudder was increased in size the same as the R–1. A new longer wing was built for the 1933 R–2, and it was fitted with flaps—the first Gee Bee to be so fitted. The plane was flown in the Bendix race from New York to Indianapolis by Russell Thaw, who withdrew from the race after witnessing Russell Boardman's crash in the R–1.

The Gee Bee R-1/R-2 Long Tail Racer

In late 1933, Jimmy Haizlip rolled the R-2 into a ball of wreckage during a landing at Springfield. Therefore, the R-1/R-2 was born. It consisted of the repaired fuselage of the R-1 which was stretched twenty-four inches over the original. A conventional tail was added and a tail skid substituted for the tail wheel. The wings of the 1932 R-2 were still available, so they were attached to the craft. To avoid repainting the wings, the craft became race number 7 even though the fuselage was from the 1933 number 11. Before it could be raced at the 1933 Chicago International Air Races, it was taxied into a ditch by West Coast race pilot Roy Minor. It was not raced in 1934.

Cecil Allen's R-1/R-2

The long-tailed racer was modified by Cecil Allen for the 1935 Bendix race after purchasing it from the Granvilles. His changes included the addition of a fuel tank far aft in the fuselage that altered the center of gravity to the point the ship was totally unstable. In addition, he eliminated the scalloped wing design, substituting just a red leading edge. The cockpit enclosure was modified to allow greater visibility. The craft crashed on take-off, killing Allen, and was totally destroyed.

The Gee Bee Racing Car

This effort in late 1933 was to build a car for the 1934 Indianapolis 500. It was teardrop in shape and three-wheeled. A large vertical fin was at the rear. Its specifications were as follows:

Wheelbase—122.5 inches
Tread, front wheels—56 inches
Overall length—227 inches
Overall width—64.5 inches
Height at rudder—84 inches
Height at cabin—64 inches
Seat width—40 inches
Turning radius—19.5 feet
Empty weight—1,750 pounds
Racing weight—2,500 pounds

The car never got off the drawing board as Eddie Rickenbacker told them it would have to be a four-wheeler to compete at Indy.

The Gee Bee Eightster

This is an example of the planning for a commercial aircraft by the Granville organization. Though this aircraft was started through the Granville shops in 1933, it was never completed due to the firm's bankruptcy. The data pertains to the ship as it would have been. It was a high-speed transport to be used on a new airline from Boston to New York. It was representative of two other design thoughts they had along the same lines—the Fourster and the Sixter. Its specifications were as follows:

Wing span—45 feet
Wing area—390 square feet
Overall length—34 feet
Empty weight—3,925 pounds
Gross weight—7,000 pounds
Powerplant—700 horsepower Wright Cyclone or Pratt and
  Whitney Wasp
Maximum speed—225 miles per hour
Cruising speed—190 miles per hour
Landing speed with flaps—50 miles per hour
Landing speed without flaps—65 miles per hour
Initial rate of climb—2,500 feet per minute
Range—870 miles or 4.5 hours
Fuel capacity—200 gallons split evenly between two wing
  tanks
Wing loading—17 pounds per square foot
Power loading—10 pounds per horsepower

The cabin dimensions were 12 feet long by 5 feet 5 inches wide. The ceiling was to be 5 feet high. There was also a compartment for 400 pounds of luggage. While the initial design featured a wire braced wing, the final design that was under construction had a full cantilever wing—a first for Granville design theory.

The Gee Bee Q.E.D. R6H

The Q.E.D. was the last Granville design and was built for Jackie Cochran to use in the Mac Robertson London to Melbourne Race of 1934. Painted Lucky Strike green, it was licensed NR14307 and later NX14307. The design was a derivative of the Gee Bee International Sportster Model R–5 which was never built. The R–5 specifications, however, were determined and a three-view drawing made. They were as follows:

Wing span—30 feet
Overall length—22 feet 6 inches

Height—8 feet 4 inches
Empty weight—2,200 pounds
Gross weight—5,040 pounds
Powerplant—825 horsepower Pratt and Whitney Hornet
Maximum speed—295 miles per hour
Cruising speed—260 miles per hour
Landing speed—50 miles per hour
Initial rate of climb—4,000 feet per minute

Jackie Cochran saw this design and, after some negotiations, the Q.E.D. was built for her. The Q.E.D. had the following performance and dimensional specifications:

Wing span—34 feet 3 inches
Wing area—211 square feet
Length overall—27 feet 2 inches
Height overall—9 feet 6 inches
Powerplant—675 horsepower Pratt and Whitney Hornet
Fuel capacity—400 gallons
Oil capacity—28 gallons
Empty weight—3,144 pounds
Gross weight—6,500 pounds
Wing loading—36 pounds per square foot

Other data that applies to the Q.E.D. are as follows:

Aileron area—21.2 square feet
Elevator area—21.2 square feet
Angle of incidence—2 degrees
Dihedral angle—4.5 degrees
Stabilizer area—24.5 square feet
Fin area—3.7 square feet
Rudder area—10.5 square feet

The Q.E.D. did not do well in the Bendix race of 1934 where it sported orange racing number 77, nor in the subsequent Mac Robertson race where it got only as far as Bucharest.

Charles Babb Q.E.D.

The Q.E.D. was purchased by Charles Babb for a try at the 1938 Bendix race. It was completely overhauled and painted a light cream with green racing stripes along the fuselage sides and wheel pants. A new 875 horsepower Pratt and Whitney Hornet engine was installed. Due to several mechanical problems, it never completed the 1938 Bendix race.

Sarabia "Conquistador del Cielo"

The Q.E.D. was purchased by Sarabia, a Mexican air hero and repainted white with red stripes down the fuselage sides and wheel pants. The ship set a speed/distance record from Mexico City to New York in 1939. On the return trip to Mexico, it crashed into the Potomac River, killing Sarabia. Its license number was XB–AKM. The plane survives in a restored form to this day in a museum in Cuidad Lerdo, Mexico.

Time Flies

Time Flies was a Gee Bee without the Gee Bee name. It was built almost identical to the other Gee Bees—right down to the streamlined teardrop fuselage. Gee Bee designer and engineer Howell Miller was the creator of this masterpiece of aerodynamic art. He was responsible for the design engineering of the Gee Bee R–1 and R–2, the long-tail hybrid and, of course, the Q.E.D. This was his first solo shot at designing a speed plane but the Gee Bee background holds forth in an unmistakable manner. Data for *Time Flies* are as follows:

Wing span—30 feet 4 inches
Wing area—160 square feet
Overall length—23 feet 6 inches
Powerplant—Pratt and Whitney R–1830 Twin Wasp delivering 1,150 horsepower. Special permission had to be obtained from the Army Air Corps to use it.
Stabilizer span—10 feet
Landing gear track—10 feet 6 inches
Angle of incidence—2.5 degrees

The color scheme of *Time Flies* was all white with blue markings. The license number was NR1313. The aircraft never did the job it was hoped it could do. This was not because it couldn't, but more because the man that handled it, Hawks, was over the hill as far as daring and skill were concerned.

Military Aircraft HM–1

The HM–1 is the final machine to be included in the Gee Bee Data Bank. It was the rebuilt remains of *Time Flies*. The idea was to build a lightweight fighter/attack aircraft that had amazing speed and performance. *Time Flies* was so modified with a two-seat cockpit covered with an AT–6 type canopy. Dimensionally, it was the same as *Time Flies*. The color scheme was changed to a black fuselage with yellow/gold wings and horizontal tail surfaces. The new license number was NX2491 and, for racing purposes, the number 41 was affixed. Flown by Leigh Wade in the 1938 Thompson, the plane did poorly. Afterward, it crashed during a series of test flights while being piloted by Earl Ortman.

THE RACES

Two major unlimited races dominated the racing scene during the Nationals of the 1930's. The first was the cross-country event, the Bendix Trophy Race. It was founded to encourage long-leggedness and endurance in the aircraft and to entice the contestants to get the maximum performance from their entries in terms of obtaining long distances covered in a minimum of time. The other race, the Thompson Trophy Race, was conceived based upon a different set of parameters. It was to get the greatest possible speed out of its contestants around a closed course with distance only of minor importance.

The Thompson Trophy Race

The Thompson Trophy Race was established in 1930 by Charles Edwin Thompson, founder of the Cleveland-based Thompson Products, Inc., to encourage speed flying. It followed on the heels of the Thompson Cup Race of 1929 in which Doug Davis in the Travel Air Mystery Ship severely trounced the military racing entrants. That also marked the beginning of the Golden Age of air racing. The Thompson Trophy Race offered a first prize of $5,000 plus the trophy in 1930. This amount more or less grew annually to $22,000 by 1938, making the money involved as rewarding as the national fame derived from winning the race. The trophy itself was kept in the winner's possession for ten months from the date of winning the race. For permanent possession, the winner received a gold plaque for first place, a silver plaque for second and a bronze plaque for third place. Frederick C. Crawford, the executive that succeeded Mr. Thompson, was as enthusiastic about the program as was his predecessor. Under the impetus of the contest, winning speeds rose steadily from about 200 miles per hour in 1939—about a thirty percent increase. The races were continued after World War II, 1946 through 1949, with cut-down, disarmed military aircraft careening around the course and, as usual, this was a free-for-all unlimited event. Just get the speed up!

The Bendix Trophy Race

Starting in 1931, this unlimited free-for-all cross-country race was sponsored by the Bendix Aviation Corporation under the leadership of its president, Vincent Bendix. It was predicated on the philosophy of encouraging experimental work toward the development of higher cross-country speeds and new transcontinental speed records. The contesting entries could be any type of aircraft and could fly the course nonstop, or with fuel stops, and even air-to-air refueling if so desired. The shortest elapsed time over the course, usually Los Angeles to Cleveland, was the method of determining the winner. Prize money for first place started out at $7,500 in 1931 and rose to $12,500 by 1939. The trophy remained in the possession of the winner for ten months (as in the Thompson Trophy Race). The winner was also given a smaller gold replica of the trophy for permanent possession. Silver and bronze replicas were also given to the second and third place winners.

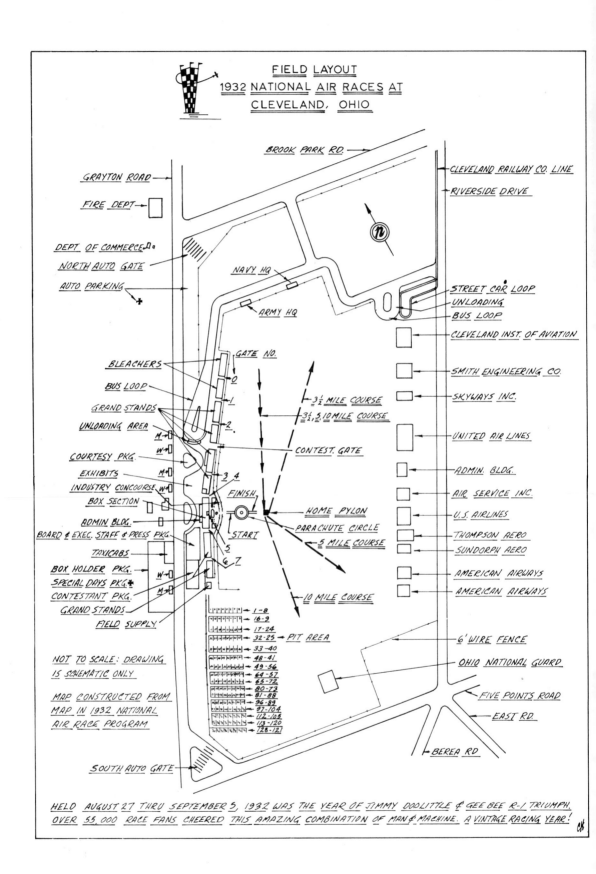

FIELD LAYOUT
1932 NATIONAL AIR RACES AT CLEVELAND, OHIO

BROOK PARK RD.

GRAYTON ROAD

FIRE DEPT

DEPT. OF COMMERCE
NORTH AUTO GATE
AUTO PARKING

NAVY HQ

ARMY HQ

GATE NO.
0
1
2

BLEACHERS
BUS LOOP
GRAND STANDS
UNLOADING AREA

COURTESY PKG.
EXHIBITS
INDUSTRY CONCOURSE
BOX SECTION
ADMIN BLDG.
BOARD & EXEC. STAFF & PRESS PKG.
TAXICABS
BOX HOLDER PKG.
SPECIAL DAYS PKG.
CONTESTANT PKG.
GRAND STANDS
FIELD SUPPLY

3 4
FINISH
5
START
6 7

M
W
M
W

W
M

CLEVELAND RAILWAY CO. LINE
RIVERSIDE DRIVE

STREET CAR LOOP
UNLOADING
BUS LOOP
CLEVELAND INST. OF AVIATION

SMITH ENGINEERING CO.

SKYWAYS INC.

UNITED AIR LINES

ADMIN. BLDG.

AIR SERVICE INC.

U.S. AIRLINES

THOMPSON AERO

SUNDORPH AERO

AMERICAN AIRWAYS

AMERICAN AIRWAYS

3½ MILE COURSE
3½, 5,10 MILE COURSE

CONTEST. GATE

HOME PYLON
PARACHUTE CIRCLE
5 MILE COURSE

10 MILE COURSE

1-8
16-9
17-24
32-25 → PIT AREA
33-40
48-41
49-56
64-57
65-72
80-73
81-88
96-89
97-104
112-105
113-120
128-121

NOT TO SCALE: DRAWING
IS SCHEMATIC ONLY

MAP CONSTRUCTED FROM
MAP IN 1932 NATIONAL
AIR RACE PROGRAM

6' WIRE FENCE

OHIO NATIONAL GUARD

FIVE POINTS ROAD

EAST RD.

BEREA RD.

SOUTH AUTO GATE

HELD AUGUST 27 THRU SEPTEMBER 5, 1932 WAS THE YEAR OF JIMMY DOOLITTLE & GEE BEE R-1 TRIUMPH.
OVER 55,000 RACE FANS CHEERED THIS AMAZING COMBINATION OF MAN & MACHINE. A VINTAGE RACING YEAR!

CK

THOMPSON TROPHY RACE

Year	Pilot	Aircraft	Speed	Year	Pilot	Aircraft	Speed
1929	Davis	Travel Air Model R	194.9	**1930**	Holman	Laird "Solution"	201.9
	Breene	Curtiss Hawk P-3A	186.8		Haizlip	Travel Air Model R	199.8
	Turner	Lockheed "Vega"	163.8		Howard	Howard "Pete"	162.8
					Adams	Travel Air Biplane	142.6
1931	Bayles	Gee Bee Model Z	236.2	**1932**	Doolittle	Gee Bee R-1	252.7
	Wedell	Wedell-Williams "44"	228.0		Wedell	Wedell-Williams "44"	242.5
	Jackson	Laird "Solution"	211.2		Turner	Wedell-Williams "57"	233.0
	Hall	Gee Bee Model Y	201.3		Haizlip	Wedell-Williams "92"	231.3
	Eaker	Lockheed Altair	196.8		Gehlbach	Gee Bee R-2	222.1
	Howard	Howard "Pete"	163.6		Hall	Hall "Bulldog"	215.6
	Ong	Laird Speedwing	153.0		Ong	Howard "Ike"	191.1
	Doolittle	Laird "Super Solution"	—				
1933	Wedell	Wedell-Williams "44"	237.9	**1934**	Turner	Wedell-Williams "57"	248.1
	Gehlbach	Wedell-Williams "92"	224.9		Minor	Brown B-2	214.9
	Minor	Howard "Mike"	199.9		Worthen	Wedell Williams "45"	208.4
	Hague	Keith Rider R-2	183.2		Neumann	Howard "Ike"	207.1
	Granville	Gee Bee Model Y	173.1		Rae	Keith Rider R-1	205.4
					Chester	Chester "Jeep"	191.6
1935	Neumann	Howard "Mr. Mulligan"	220.2	**1936**	Detroyat	Caudron C-460	264.3
	Wittman	Wittman "Bonzo"	218.7		Ortman	Keith Rider R-3	248.0
	Rae	Keith-Rider R-1	213.9		Rae	Keith Rider R-4	236.6
	Jacobson	Howard "Mike"	209.1		Neumann	Folkerts "Toots"	233.1
	Miles	Seversky SEV-3	193.6		McKeen	Brown B-2	230.5
	McKeen	Brown B-2	188.9		Crosby	Crosby Special CR-3	226.1
	Turner	Wedell-Williams "57"					
1937	Kling	Folkerts "Jupiter"	256.9	**1938**	Turner	Laird-Turner LTR-14	283.4
	Ortman	Marcoux Bromberg R-3	256.8		Ortman	Marcoux Bromberg R-3	269.7
	Turner	Laird-Turner LTR-14	253.8		Wittman	Wittman "Bonzo"	259.1
	Sinclair	Seversky SEV-S2	252.4		Wade	HM-1 (Time Flies)	249.8
	Wittman	Wittman "Bonzo"	250.1		Mackey	Wedell-Williams "57"	249.6
	Moore	Seversky SEV-S2	238.4		Jacobson	Keith-Rider "8 Ball"	214.5
	Gotch	Schoenfeldt "Firecracker"	217.8				

BENDIX TROPHY RACE

Year	Pilot	Aircraft	Speed	Year	Pilot	Aircraft	Speed
1931	Doolittle	Laird "Super Solution"	223.0	**1932**	Haizlip	Wedell-Williams "92"	245
	Johnson	Lockheed Orion	198.8		Wedell	Wedell-Williams "44"	232
	Blevins	Lockheed Orion	189.0		Turner	Wedell-Williams "57"	226
	Eaker	Lockheed Altair	186.1		Gehlbach	Gee Bee R-2	210
					Vance	Vance Flying Wing	—
1933	Turner	Wedell-Williams "57"	214.8	**1934**	Davis	Wedell-Williams "44"	216.2
	Wedell	Wedell-Williams "44"	209.2		Worthen	Wedell-Williams "92"	203.2
	Boardman	Gee Bee R-1	—		Gehlbach	Gee Bee QED	—
	Thaw	Gee Bee R-2	—				
	Gehlbach	Wedell-Williams "92"	—				
	Earhart	Lockheed "Vega"	—				
1935	Neumann-			**1936**	Thaden-Noyes	Beech C-17	165.3
	Howard	Howard "Mr. Mulligan"	238.7		Ingalls	Lockheed "Orion"	157.5
	Turner	Wedell-Williams "57"	238.5		Bulick	Vultee VIA-1	156.5
	Thaw	Northrup "Gamma"	201.9		Pomeroy	Douglas DC-2	151.5
	Hunt	Lockheed "Orion"	174.8		Earhart	Lockheed "Electra"	148.7
					Howard-Wife	Howard "Mr. Mulligan"	—
					Jacobson	Northrup "Gamma"	—
					Miles	Gee Bee "QED"	—
1937	Fuller	Seversky SEV-S2 (P-35)	258.2	**1938**	Cochran	Seversky SEV-S2	249.7
	Ortman	Marcoux Bromberg R-3	224.8		Fuller	Seversky SEV-S2	238.6
	Cochran	Beech "Straggerwing"	194.7		Mantz	Lockheed "Orion"	206.6
	Sinclair	Seversky SEV-S2	184.9		Constant	Beech "Staggerwing"	199.3
	Burcham	Lockheed 12	184.5		Hadley	Beech "Staggerwing"	181.8
	Sundorph	Sundorph A-1	166.2		LaJatte	Spartan 7W	177.4
	Perlick	Beech Staggerwing A17F	—		Armistead	Gee Bee "QED"	—
	Mackey	Wedell-Williams "44"			Perlick	Beech A-17F	—
					Cordova	Bellanca Trimotor	—

Index

Bibliography

Air Progress. *World's Great Aircraft*. Los Angeles: Petersen Publishing Co., 1972.

The American Heritage History of Flight. New York: American Heritage Publishing Co., 1962.

Bowers, Peter M. *The Gee Bee Racers Profile 51*. London: Profile Publications Ltd., 1965.

Buehl, F. and H. Gann. *National Air Race Sketchbook*. Los Angeles: Floyd Clymer, 1949.

Christy, Joe. *Racing Planes Guide*. New York: Sports Car Press, 1963.

Cooke, David C. *Racing Planes That Made History*. New York: G. P. Putnam Sons, 1960.

Kinert, Reed. *American Racing Planes and Historic Air Races*. Chicago: Wilcox & Follet Co., 1952.

Kinert, Reed. *Racing Planes and Air Races*, V. 1-6. Fallbrook, California: Aero Publishers, 1969.

Mandrake, Charles G. *The Gee Bee Story*. Wichita, Kansas: Robert R. Longo Co., 1957.

Mandrake, Charles G. *National Air Races 1932, A Pictorial Review*. Speed Publishing, 1976.

Mendenhall, Charles A. *The Air Racer 1909-1975*. Rochester, New York: Pylon Publications, 1976.

Thomas, Lowell and Edward Jablonski. *Doolittle—A Biography*. Garden City, New York: Doubleday and Co., 1976.

Underwood, John W. *The World's Famous Racing Aircraft*. Los Angeles: Floyd Clymer, 1949.

Vorderman, Don. *The Great Air Races*. Garden City, New York: Doubleday and Co., 1969.

Weaver, Truman C. and S. H. Schmid. *The Golden Age of Air Racing—Pre 1940*. Hales Corners, Wisconsin: EAA Air Museum Foundation, 1963.

Weaver, Truman C. *62 Rare Racing Planes From The Golden Years of Aviation*. New York: Arenar Publications.

Wings and Airpower. Granada Hills, California: monthly 1971 to date.

Photo by Robert L. Hogeman

Charles A. Mendenhall has done articles and illustrations for several aviation magazines in addition to his previous book, *The Air Racer*. He is a member of Aviation/Space Writers Association. His mainstream activity is that of automotive engineer where he has accumulated twenty-two patents.